Muriel James, coauthor of the bestseller, *Born To Win*, has been a pioneer in Transactional Analysis and Gestalt Therapy since 1958, and worked closely with the late Dr. Eric Berne, the originator of IA.

Using TA concepts, Dr. James explains how our bossing style is related to certain "OK" and "not-OK" aspects of our personality. She tells how our OK sides can be nurtured and developed to make us better bosses, feel better about being bossed, and bring about changes in the way people boss us.

Dr. James received her doctorate from the University of California at Berkeley, and has since been an adviser to the California Commission on the Status of Women, has trained consultants and faculty members at numerous universities, and has lectured throughout the world as an international consultant in Transactional Analysis. She is vice president of the International Transactional Analysis Association, director of the Transactional Analysis Association in Lafayette, California, and a licensed marriage and family counselor.

Bantam Books by Muriel James

BORN TO LOVE
THE OK BOSS

THE
OK BOSS

MURIEL JAMES

Human Relations and
Communications Consultant
Lafayette, California

•

Illustrations by
John Trotta

BANTAM BOOKS · TORONTO · NEW YORK · LONDON

THE OK BOSS

*A Bantam Book / published by arrangement with
Addison-Wesley Publishing Company, Inc.*

PRINTING HISTORY

Addison-Wesley edition published October 1975
2nd printing ...... December 1975   3rd printing ...... February 1976

A condensation appeared in PSYCHOLOGY TODAY,
February 1976 under the title "The OK Boss in All of Us"

Bantam edition / September 1977

To my husband, Ernest Brawley,
Who bosses me with confidence and strength,
With tenderness and warmth,
And gives me "equal opportunity"
To do the same with him.

Acknowledgments

To my friends and colleagues in the International Transactional Analysis Association, my greetings and thanks. I have learned from you and deeply appreciate the relationship.

In particular, thanks to you, Steve Karpman, for your concept of the drama triangle. Thanks to you, John James, for your concept of the game plan. Thanks to you, Aaron and Jacqui Schiff, for your concept of discounting. And thanks to you, Claude Steiner, for your concept of warm fuzzies and cold pricklies.

If you, the reader, are interested in training or consulting with me, write to the Oasis Transactional Analysis Institute or write to Muriel James Associates, Inc., Box 356, Lafayette, California 94949.

If you are interested in other accredited trainers, therapists, or educators, or wish information on other Transactional Analysis literature, write to the International Transactional Analysis Association, 1772 Vallejo Street, San Francisco, California 94123.

Lafayette, California   M.J.
August 1975

Contents

THE
OK BOSS

Introduction

At one time or another, almost everyone is a boss. Parents are seen as bosses. So are spouses, teachers, and employers. All the way up the ladder, somebody usually bosses somebody else, or at least wants to boss them. As one seven-year-old said, "Mom, I wish you'd have another baby quick. I'm tired of emptying the garbage. If there was someone else in this family, I'd boss them around and tell *them* to do it!"

I firmly believe that everyone wants to be an OK boss. This book will show how to become one using the techniques of Transactional Analysis (TA), a clear, reasonable theory that can be applied immediately. TA offers a fresh way of looking at the traditional functions of bosses— setting goals, reducing conflict, establishing priorities, increasing productivity, and coping with crisis. Also, TA will help you and others enjoy life more, both on and off the job.

This book will also increase your awareness of what it takes to become an OK boss. You will learn:

■ to recognize the bossing styles of others, as well as your own.

■ to find out why bosses (and other people) act the way they do.

■ to discover OK and not-OK attitudes at work and at home.

■ to understand the importance of giving (and getting!) positive recognition.

■ to improve communication on the job.

■ to detect games people play in work situations.

■ to identify psychological scripts—what they are and how they affect people within an organization.

■ to establish contracts for personal and interpersonal positive change.

Each chapter includes a "Self-Discovery" exercise to help you become more aware of yourself as a boss, a section called "So What to Do" which provides practical suggestions for change, and a third section which provides a guide for effective and efficient bossing.

Becoming an OK boss isn't always easy. But it can be fun. Hopefully, this book will show you how it can be done. It is intended to make so much sense that before you know it, you will be increasing the basic OKness you already have.

1

Styles
of
OK bosses

Bosses are not always bossy

The word "boss" is a colloquial term for master. In business it is used for those who have others under their direction or control. It does not mean the same as a phrase which denotes skill, such as "master craftsman." The word "boss" stresses *authority* rather than capacity. It is used for supervisors, managers, and top executives by those who feel *under* that particular person. It is seldom used for a subordinate except as a derogatory adjective when one person criticizes another for being "bossy."

Traditionally, the supervisor's job is considered the management of people and the solving of problems related to their particular jobs. The manager's job is generally more diversified. It is to set objectives, to organize personnel and resources in order to achieve these objectives, and to establish ways of measuring the degree of success or failure. It is also the manager's job to motivate and communicate with people, and to develop their skills.

In actual practice, the supervisors, managers, top executives, corporation officers, and board of directors all deal with people—both as bosses and as subordinates. Each has a boss responsibility *for* someone else. Each has a boss responsibility *to* someone else. Even corporation officers have to please others—the board of directors, the stockholders, and, ultimately, the consumers—if the organization is to survive. They don't always enjoy doing it.

Learning how to be an OK boss is not an easy task. Although some people seem to be able to do it more easily than others, the reasons why are not always clear.

OK bosses are continually in the process of evaluating themselves so that they can become more self-actualizing. They are committed to what they consider to be worthwhile work. They are doers as well as dreamers, pioneers as well as planners. Their work is part of their identity, and both their work and personhood contribute to their own well-being and the productivity of others.

They do not wait passively for things to happen. They are motivators and agents of change who initiate events. Instead of wasting their time, they use it creatively and productively. In essence, they're bright. They would agree with Maslow, who said, "What is not worth doing is not worth doing well."

Bossing Styles

There are many typical styles of boss behavior that can conveniently be regarded as stereotypes. People seldom fit a stereotype because stereotypes, by definition, lack originality and each person is an "original," not a copy of anyone else. Nevertheless, stereotypes are often useful, like a mirror which distorts images while still reflecting some of the truth.

Many OK and not-OK people have similar personality traits but use the traits in different ways. For example, some bosses have the personality characteristics of a *Critic*: they judge, discern, discuss, and communicate. From their OK side, these bosses are *Informed Critics*; from their not-OK side, they become *Critical Dictators*.

Here are some common styles of boss behavior found in many organizations. Each behavior style has its not-OK side and its OK side:

The critic: From not-OK Critical Dictator to OK Informed Critic

The coach: From not-OK Benevolent Dictator to OK Supportive Coach

The shadow: From not-OK Loner to OK Liberator

The analyst: From not-OK Computer to OK Communicator

The pacifier: From not-OK Milquetoast to OK-Negotiator

The fighter: From not-OK Punk to OK Partner

The inventor: From not-OK Scatterbrain to OK Innovator

Most bosses have a favorite bossing style. At one time or another, however, all bosses find themselves acting out each of these stereotypes.

The Critic:
From critical dictator to informed critic

Critics, according to Webster, are those who express a reasoned opinion involving a value judgment. They are able to discuss, judge, discern, and communicate.

From their not-OK side, Critics become *Dictators*; nagging, repressive, or opinionated parental-type bosses who insist that things go their way. Critical Dictators are seldom open to new ideas or new procedures. "That's the way it's always been and that's the way it's going to be," claims this type of boss.

If a change in product, program, or services seems necessary, the changes made are often extensions of the Critical Dictator's previously held traditions and prejudices. If changes happen that the Dictator is not in favor of, then he or she may undermine the progress with the strongly held belief, "I know more than they do."

The *Informed Critic*, however, is quite different. Like a good theatrical critic who evaluates a stage play with competence, an Informed Critic, while on the job, does the same.

In their discussions, Informed Critics are open-minded while discussing the pros and cons. They are capable of communicating clearly, whether talking or writing. They listen carefully and accurately when receiving verbal communications. They are also quick to spot nonverbal messages.

Like Solomon, they withhold making judgments until the facts are available. Informed Critics have the ability to discern between the important and the unimportant. Because of their powers of discernment, they often stress accuracy.

Critics have great value in every kind of organization. They are the ones who often insist on getting things done and getting them done on time. They work well under pressure and pull things together when the pieces "hit the fan."

Such bosses often expect a lot from people and, consequently, may get a lot. They also tend to maintain traditions, many of which are useful. They set limits so that employees know what is expected. This provides a sense of security.

Critics may not be as socially popular as other types because of their critiquing ability. Coworkers may label this bossing style "over critical," and may call such persons "drivers," or "Little Napoleons." But critics are usually respected for what they accomplish.

A strong Critic is often a potent OK boss.

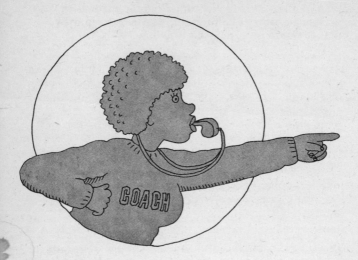

The Coach:
From benevolent dictator to supportive coach

Coaches are supportive, Parental-type bosses who often take pleasure in caring for their employees.

From their not-OK side, Coaches become *Benevolent Dictators*. They overwhelm and manipulate employees with their concern. This type of boss, like the Critical Dictator, often, with good intentions, insists on things going his or her way. To effect this, such a boss may be overly helpful. This attitude encourages helpless and dependent responses.

A Benevolent Dictator's desire to be helpful may be hidden behind remarks such as, "You really do well when you put your mind to it," or "I'm sure you can do it if you just try harder," or "Let me finish it for you," or "I'll put someone else on the job. You've been working so hard." Underneath the overnurturing mask there is sometimes the paternalistic, condescending attitude of a person who feels threatened with other people's talents or achievements, and thus helps to "keep them in their place."

A more positive use of these caring and encouraging personality traits is found in those bosses who act as *Supportive Coaches*. They encourage their coworkers as an athletic coach might do. They cheer others on. They give pep talks. They do everything possible to help employees develop to their fullest potential and are pleased with their successes. Supportive Coaches are often concerned over issues such as fair employment practices and the physical and emotional health of coworkers.

They are usually patient when giving instructions. They will repeat instructions if not understood. They are flexible and willing to change their plan of action if it seems appropriate.

From their OK side, Coaches are often very competent at motivating employees. They can listen well and give active feedback. They are supportive and give appropriate advice and sympathy. As a consequence, other employees tend to feel understood by the Coach and, because they feel understood, often respond with higher motivation and productivity.

Supportive Coaches are disliked by some employees for their overnurturing ways. They are labeled "too amiable" or "too buddy-buddy." Others, however, appreciate this type of boss precisely for those care-taking qualities.

The Shadow:
From loner to liberator

Shadows have little substance. They are one-dimensional, therefore difficult to grasp. Neither critical nor nurturing, they stay uninvolved.

From their not-OK side, Shadows are *Loner* bosses. Such bosses often use a closed door, a large wide desk, and a tip-back chair for themselves. The chairs for others who necessarily come in are often set at a distance or are uncomfortable enough to convey a "don't stay" message.

Loners act unconcerned over the well-being of their employees. Sometimes they are intellectuals who may succeed in the academic life while they fail at an inter-personal level. It is not unusual for a research scientist to be "advanced" to a boss position. Often, accustomed to working alone on a project, such a person may continue as a Loner and a Shadow unless he or she gets training in supervision or management skills.

On the positive side, Shadow bosses may really be *Liberators*. Because they do not interfere, other people are free to "do their own thing," work at their own pace, set their own limits, design their own goals, run their own show, and develop their own program.

Noninterfering Liberators "stay out of the way" and tend to maintain a "hands-off" policy with employees. For example, they may not insist that their top sales personnel attend pep-talk sales meetings or give reports on schedule. They are seldom either overly helpful or repressive.

Liberators often expect others to be creative, trustworthy, and competent. It is not surprising that they often get their expected response. Whereas dependent-type people may want and need stronger Parental leadership, the self-motivated, self-starter employee will thrive in the liberating atmosphere of an OK Shadow boss.

Shadows are loner bosses.
Such bosses often use
a closed door, a large
wide desk, and tip-back
chair for themselves.

The Analyst:
From computer to communicator

The always-rational Analyst is continually adding and subtracting, multiplying and dividing—products, numbers, and people.

From their not-OK side, Analysts become *Computers*, primarily intent on processing data, especially data related to economics. They are often inadequate in dealing with the human side of supervision and management because they focus too much on computing statistics.

Computers seldom show sympathy and concern unless the concern might in some way lead to economic profit.

They may say things like, "The job is no place to discuss personal problems," or "Let's not talk about personal matters. Let's get on with the job." If they don't speak this way, it won't change anything, they frequently think it.

If Computers attend a company, department, or agency party, they often buttonhole someone to discuss dollars and cents. They may act as if they had lost the ability to laugh and play, and tend to leave early if the party becomes fun, or stay and observe objectively while remaining uninvolved.

The positive flip side of a mechanistic Computer is a responsive *Communicator*. This is a very potent boss who is strong because of this same ability to collect data, analyze it, and estimate probabilities.

This boss is humanistically oriented; people are important. Decisions are made that include this basic value. The responsive Communicator works on speaking and writing clearly, and is not redundant, vague, evasive, or inconsistent.

Communicator bosses use time productively because they know the importance of clear communication. They do not get caught up in psychological games such as, *Now I've Got You, You S.O.B.*, or *If It Weren't For Him*, or *Look How Hard I'm Trying*. They know that there's a time for work and a time for play and how to distinguish between the two.

Sometimes coworkers are jealous of Communicator bosses who seem to have it all together and tend to say it well. They may accuse them of being "too analytical." As a rule, however, such bosses are appreciated for the clear way in which they think and act.

The Pacifier:
From milquetoast to negotiator

Pacifier bosses are generally "agreeable." They provide a soothing, balanced atmosphere at work.

The obedient, compliant, always agreeing, Childlike boss is a scared *Milquetoast*, a doormat. Soft, bland, often boring, Milquetoast bosses usually give in both to superiors and subordinates. They seldom speak up on their own behalf. Instead, they act servile and try to please everyone, though they seldom succeed.

Such bosses are also fearful of conflict. They will go to great lengths to avoid a head-on confrontation, saying such things as, "Let's not get upset," or "It will all work out in time," or "Arguing won't get us anywhere." As a result, some problems never get solved as they are never "battled" through.

The agreeableness of Pacifier bosses is positive on the flip side. It has a strong healing quality and is a crucial characteristic of a fair *Negotiator*. The balm is especially useful when tempers are high and permanent alienation could result from the fighting.

The Negotiator often provides a balanced atmosphere for employees who like to work on their own. He or she can be counted on not to "rock the boat" too hard, or totally "upset the applecart," or carelessly "muddy the waters."

Because of a seeming willingness to examine the other side of most disputes and to sometimes "go along with" other people's opinions, coworkers often feel as if they can relax and let down their defenses in the presence of fair Negotiator bosses. Consequently, there is more opportunity for misunderstandings to be clarified, conflicts to be negotiated, and problems to be solved.

The Fighter:
From punk to partner

Fighter bosses are aggressive. They actively pursue success.

The sulky, rebellious, hostile, Childlike boss is like a *Punk* who fights crooked. Certain kinds of golfers, called "sandbaggers," are also like this; they are crooked about their score and manage to get a higher handicap than they deserve, thus gaining an unfair advantage. They're out to win by any means, fair or foul.

This kind of boss has a lot of hostility, which may or may not be openly expressed. Sulkiness, for example, is a disguised form of hostility. It is expressed by Punk bosses who, for example, procrastinate in setting vacation schedules, establishing budgets, discussing personnel problems, and so forth.

When hostility is more open, it may be expressed as an excessive competitiveness which so permeates the environment that it is felt by others to be an invasion.

When things go wrong, the Punk goes for revenge: "I'm going to get her fired," or "You tell that client that we don't care about his business." Often people like this are in an "I win, you lose" position. They act as if there's not enough to go around so they have to have it all— highest salary, title, and so forth.

Fighter bosses also have strong positive value when they channel their assertiveness toward teamwork. They act as good business *Partners* with their employees. This kind of boss will fight for success, will often defend the company against competitors, and will struggle to protect the department and its budget and personnel against so-called attackers.

The negative hostility of a crooked Fighter is positively expressed as "guts" by a Partner.

As fair assertive Partners, such bosses share information with their employees, clue them in on new strategies and techniques, develop a positive fighting team spirit among them, and act as OK referees if necessary.

They never keep pertinent information secret. They continually update others on new developments. Out of a sense of fairness, they act with integrity and refuse to take an unfair advantage over others.

The Inventor:
From scatterbrain to innovator

Inventors often have a flair for genius. Their new ideas come quickly and easily.

Scatterbrains are often so busy being experimental that they do not allot the time and energy necessary to complete a task. They often do not have the communication skills necessary to make their creative ideas understood and adopted. "Let's try something new" is their constant refrain.

Some Scatterbrains work in relative isolation, then come out from behind the door to "spring" their new ideas on others. Others continually interact, hoping people will approve of their schemes.

This same exciting flair for new ideas is positively expressed in the creative *Innovator*. This boss provides an exciting atmosphere.

Such people are often well liked for their ready flow of fresh ideas and enthusiasm that energize others. "I've got a great idea," they might say, "*and* I think I know how we could do it." They are sometimes great joke-tellers, creative clowns, the life of any party, intuiting a natural desire in other people to be entertained. Inventors can usually be counted on to dream up new solutions for old problems, new designs for outmoded equipment, and new policies, programs, and procedures for others to implement.

Whereas some subordinates are uncomfortable with a boss who's always coming up with new ideas for products, services, or marketing, others find it stimulating. It releases their own basic creativity. They feel alive and ready to go.

Self-discovery 1

At one time or another, most people find themselves acting in each of the bossing styles listed below. How about you? On a continuum of minus to plus:

1. How might you rate your boss?

2. How would you rate yourself as a boss?

3. How might your subordinates rate you?

The critic

critical dictator	not-ok		ok	informed critic
	100%	0	100%	

The coach

benevolent dictator	not-ok		ok	competent motivator
	100%	0	100%	

The shadow

loner	not-ok		ok	liberator
	100%	0	100%	

The analyst

computer	not-ok		ok	communicator
	100%	0	100%	

The fighter

punk	not-ok		ok	partner
	100%	0	100%	

The pacifier

milquetoast	not-ok		ok	negotiator
	100%	0	100%	

The innovator

scatterbrain	not-ok		ok	inventor
	100%	0	100%	

So what to do

If you like your self-evaluation, just keep on doing what you're doing! It's evidently productive. Seemingly, you're moving towards self-actualization and helping others to realize their potentials.

If you think there is any cause for change, the easiest way is to experiment by acting from the positive side of your bossing style. Or, if you see yourself at the positive pole and perceive your boss or subordinates on the negative side, try, deliberately, to switch them.

How? Well, experiment for one week.

- Write your memos and answer your phone from your plus side.

- Say things such as "I'm glad to hear from you," or "I think that's a good plan," or "I appreciate your loyalty," or "I notice you're working hard on the project," or "I'm interested in hearing your ideas."

- In evaluations, accentuate the positive. Point out the weaknesses that need correcting, but put the stress on people's strengths.

- Operate differently in a meeting. Change your tone of voice, the words you use, your body language.

If you've found yourself with Scatterbrain characteristics, deliberately plan to present your next idea logically and coherently to your coworkers. Maybe even write the information down and refer to it so you won't get off the track.

If you're a Loner, deliberately plan to walk through your company or department saying something like, "Hi, how are you? How is your work going?"

If you seem to be a Critical Dictator, try actively listening to some new ideas. Choose one, then try it out. See what happens.

Everyone has the capacity to be an Informed Critic, a Supportive Coach, a Liberator, a Communicator, a

Partner, a Negotiator, and an Innovator. Many people are some of each, so try a different bossing style. See what happens when you approach others in a radically different way.

You will probably find that when you act more and more OK, others will respond in like manner.
If, by any chance, you're fairly well locked into a negative way of being, others will be surprised by your change. Some won't believe it; others may not even notice it. So what! Try it anyway. You've got nothing to lose and lots to gain. The emotional climate around you is bound to change. And for the better.

Effective and efficient bosses

Depending upon what his or her job is, a boss's task is either to *supervise* and improve, or *manage* and improve. Many bosses supervise, manage, and improve by optimizing the people-resources which are available.

Whereas some bosses favor one kind of bossing behavior, others flip back and forth into several of the common patterns. For example, a given boss may act like a Critical Dictator with some employees, like an Informed Critic with others, like a Supportive Coach at some times, and like a fair Negotiator at other times. And necessarily so. The ability to change is a factor in effectiveness and efficiency.

Effectiveness is doing the right thing. Most firms discover that manufacturing an outmoded product is not effective, no matter how well it may be done. For example, Model-T Fords have a certain popularity, but to open a plant to manufacture this product would hardly be effective.

Offering a service that is not wanted is also ineffective, no matter how well the service might be performed. A garage that advertises the servicing of expensive foreign cars is not effective in a small town where few such cars exist.

Whereas some bosses favor one kind of bossing behavior, others flip back and forth into several of the common patterns.

Effective firms research the market for customers' interests and needs, and then provide the appropriate services or products. Effective bosses do the same thing; they analyze the interests and needs of their subordinates or coworkers and then adjust their bossing style to motivate the people they manage or supervise.

Efficiency is doing things right. This includes examining the management and supervisional processes for strengths and weaknesses and making the appropriate changes.

Efficiency also includes knowledge of how to market a product (including oneself), and how to approach a customer or employee or even another boss. Effectiveness and efficiency go hand in hand. Both are essential for OK bosses. Having the *idea* for a good program or product is not the same as implementing it. However, if that idea isn't a sound one, then no matter how efficiently it is produced, it will still be wrong.

The *effective* boss is likely to be able to change bossing styles whenever it seems appropriate. That is doing the right thing, not getting stuck in an outmoded attitude. The *efficient* boss will make the shifts in such a way that the people involved will know that their boss is someone who cares about their well-being. That is doing things right.

Peter Drucker, in his book *Management*, claims that "Effectiveness is the foundation of success—efficiency is a minimum condition for survival *after* success has been achieved."

Doing the right thing is usually enhanced by doing it right, and that includes the OK supervision and management of OK people.

2
Personalities of OK bosses

A tool for understanding

People can be understood, subordinates can be understood, and bosses can be understood using a theory
called Transactional Analysis (TA). It was developed by
Dr. Eric Berne, best known for his book, *Games People
Play*, and was popularized by Harris's *I'm OK - You're OK*
and James and Jongeward's *Born To Win*.

TA is widely used in business, industry, and govern-
mental agencies. It is popular because it is a positive tool
that can be used to enhance life. TA is relatively easy
and fun to learn, and it can be applied immediately to
both on-the-job and off-the-job situations.

Why bosses are the way they are

According to TA, everyone's personality is composed of
three parts called *ego states*. An ego state is a system of
feelings and experiences related to a pattern of behavior.

When people, including bosses, feel and act as they did in
childhood, they are said to be in their *Child ego state*.
Each person has had unique childhood experiences.
Therefore, when acting from the Child ego state, each
person will be somewhat different.

When people, including bosses, are thinking and acting
rationally, when they are gathering facts, estimating
probabilities, and evaluating results, they are said to be in
their *Adult ego state*. Various learning experiences add to
the data stored in the Adult. These experiences affect
analytical ability. Therefore, each person's ability to think
and act rationally from the Adult ego state will also be
different.

When people, including bosses, feel and act as their
parent figures once did, they are said to be in their *Parent
ego state*. Each person has learned unique attitudes,
opinions, and prejudices from parent figures. So each
person will also be different when acting from his or her
Parent ego state.

Using ego states

At one time or another, most people exhibit all three ego-state behaviors.

To cite an example, Bill Miller was an effective computer programmer who could write and run a 150-step program while his coworkers were wondering where to start. At home, however, he was exceedingly harsh on his children, *just as his father had been with him.* In social situations Bill sometimes drank more than he could handle. Then he would have a temper tantrum and stamp his feet *as he had in childhood.* In other words, he could act from any of his ego states.

It's important to remember that it is not always best to act only from the Adult ego state. Sometimes it is appropriate, even necessary, to act from the Parent or Child ego states. If your spouse dies, you need Parental

In social situations Bill sometimes drank more than he could handle. Then he would have a temper tantrum and stamp his feet as he had in childhood

sympathy from your best friend. You don't need to hear a recital of actuary tables. And what fun would sex be if we spent our time verbally analyzing, calculating, and anatomically describing (with precision!) what gives us pleasure? With some awareness, each person can develop a good integration of the three ego states.

Ego states are diagrammed like this:

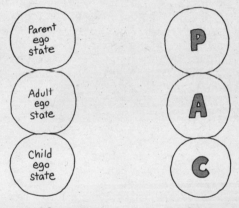

Diagram of Personality   Simplified Diagram

When the capital letters P, A, and C are used, they refer to ego states; when not capitalized, they refer to actual parents, adults, and children.

Each of the bossing stereotypes in Chapter 1 can be assigned to one of the three ego states.

The Parent ego state

The Critical Dictator and the Informed Critic, the Benevolent Dictator and the Supporting Coach, the Loner and the Liberator—all come from the Parent ego state. Many of their personality characteristics are distinctly parental.

Critical Dictators may shout others down, use absolutes such as "always" and "never," firm directives such as "you should" and "you must," and shake an accusing finger at other employees. Informed Critics may also be firm and positive about what they think, but their behavior is not intended to put others down.

Both the Benevolent Dictator and the Supportive Coach may exhibit nurturing Parental behavior by patting others on the back, looking sympathetic, and often saying things such as "don't worry, it'll be all right." The difference is that Benevolent Dictators continually hover over their employees. This overnurturing often interferes with employees' personal growth. Supportive Coaches know that people need encouragement and approval, but they don't overdo it.

Shadow bosses who are Loners or Liberators demonstrate less common Parental behavior. They are like the father or mother who is never there, either physically or emotionally.

Loners move through most situations without eye or body contact. In conversations, they tend to look away from others and show little facial expression. They often seem preoccupied. In contrast, Liberators often make real, though perhaps brief, contact with others. They say things such as "do as you think best."

The Adult ego state

The stereotype most commonly associated with the Adult ego state is the Analyst who acts as a mechanistic Computer or a responsive Communicator.

Both kinds of bosses continually ask who, what, why, when, where, and how. Their voices tend to be clear. Their posture tends to be straight rather than bent over and crooked. They are thoughtful. The difference between them is that the Loner computes like a robot; the other utilizes feedback and information. Communicators act interested in others and create a healthy atmosphere.

The Child ego state

The Child ego state is more noticeable in the Fighter who is Punk or Partner, in the Pacifier who is Milquetoast or Negotiator, and in the Inventor who is Scatterbrain or Innovator.

People who are into Punk roles may taunt and needle others, stand with their feet apart, hands on hips, chin high and a "try-and-make-me" facial expression. They learned early in life to act this way.

As assertive Partners, they may also take a fighting stance, but they are not basically hostile. Instead they act more like a member of a team. They are *for* those whom they see as partners. If they are *against* someone else, they "play fair."

Milquetoasts often look helpless, woebegone, or anxious. They tend to say "please," look worried, and scurry around straightening things. They may squirm bodily and placate constantly out of a childhood fear of not being liked.

Negotiators may also be placating. However, like Communicators, their eyes are usually alert. They watch and listen carefully to others and seldom express strong feelings. They say things such as "let's look at both sides of the problem." They say the right words at the right time to further negotiations.

Scatterbrains are like hyperkinetic children. They are very active physically. Their attention span is short. They may pace their office, go rapidly from one person's desk to another, forget their agendas, look confused and flighty, and say such things as "You lost me," or "I thought I told you that."

The creative Innovator also tends to be physically active, but looks excited instead of confused and bubbles out with ideas that hang together instead of ideas that go off like fireworks in every direction. Like a precocious child, the Innovator often breaks away from routine thinking with a new workable idea or a different way of looking at the same old problem.

Switching ego states

All bosses use their Adult ego state at times. They think and act intelligently and rationally. Some do this because the Adult is their "favorite" style. Many others enjoy using other parts of the personality *along with* their Adult.

A common mistake of many bosses and subordinates is to *believe* that they are only in their rational Adult ego state when such is not the case. Unless they have a rigid Adult ego-state boundary (and that's a problem), they are often likely to be using some of their Parent or some of their Child.

Ego-state boundaries are like semipermeable membranes. Psychic energy can flow through them from one ego state to another unless blocked off.

One of the goals in TA is to be able to shift energy from one ego state to another at will. Some bosses do it well. Some do not. If bosses do not shift energy easily, it is because of rigid ego-state boundaries, or because the Adult ego state is contaminated.

Rigid ego-state boundaries

The problem of rigid ego-state boundaries is expressed by people who have a "favorite" ego state. They constantly use one and keep the others "under control." This is diagramed as:

Parent excluding Adult and Child   Adult excluding Parent and Child   Child excluding Parent and Adult

Some people are *Constant Parents*. A Constant Parent is a person who treats others as if they were children. Such behavior can be found in the secretary who comes in early and seemingly "takes care of" everything; in the boss who tries to run the personal lives of employees; and in the person who displays little interest, involvement, or sense of humor.

Either knowingly or unknowingly, Constant Parent bosses may select people who are also Constant Parents. Together they may share the same opinions or prejudices. Or, on the other hand, they may select people who are constantly in the Child ego state. Such people get their security from being dependent, or from criticizing bosses for being "too bossy" or for not being bossy enough.

However, being the Constant Parent is not always effective in the long haul. It tends to perpetuate dependent Child responses from others.

Some bosses are *Constant Adults*. In such cases, they are consistently objective and primarily concerned with facts. They tend to select jobs that are object-oriented rather than people-oriented. They are impatient with those who "bring their personal problems to work."

Constant Adults may also prefer to be somewhat withdrawn, like Shadow bosses who are Loners. They tend to think abstractly in preference to responding forthrightly as an OK Communicator. This is also ineffective. The mechanistic thinking and behavior of most Constant Adults does not bring out the caring and creativity in others.

A few bosses are the *Constant Child*. This is the person who, like Peter Pan, doesn't want to grow up. If such people have adopted a Milquetoast style, they continually comply with others' requests. If they are Punks, they may demand, like sulky children, that things go their way. If they are Scatterbrained, they are continually "off somewhere in space" thinking up creative ideas and doing little about them.

Rigidly responding from only one ego state can be a
serious problem because all ego states have some value.
Energy needs to flow back and forth between the OK
parts of the Parent, Adult, and Child.

Employee responses to constant type bosses

The concept of a boss being bossy is often a holdover
from childhood. Many children see parents as bossy and
conclude that anyone in an authority position should or
shouldn't act that way. When they grow up, these people
tend to boss others as they themselves were bossed.
Some people modify what they perceived as children
and incorporate less of their parents' behavior. Some
reject it entirely.

Many employees respond to Constant Parents by gossiping behind their backs with resentful remarks such as
"My boss is always telling me what to do," or "My boss
is always hanging over my work and trying to 'help' when
I don't need it and don't want it," or "My boss never
talks to me, so I don't know where I stand."

Other employees, those who *prefer* a Constant Parent
boss, may say positive things such as "I may get criticized
a lot, but at least I know what my boss wants," or "My
boss is so willing to help I don't have to worry about little
mistakes," or "My boss leaves me alone to do my own
thing, and I like it."

Some employees perceive other authorities as being
mechanistic Computers, as data banks with enough
knowledge and programming to compute all factors
accurately. They may resent this and complain,
"All my boss knows is facts and figures."

If they perceive a fact-gathering boss as a Communicator,
they may affirm, "My boss listens, understands, and gives
me clear instructions."

Some employees see authorities as Punks whom they
would "like to beat up." "I'd like to get that S.O.B. in a
dark alley," they might say from behind a coffee cup. On

the other hand, some may see the positive side of a Fighter boss—that of a confident, assertive Partner who fights aggressively—and they may boast, "I like someone who sticks up for me. And my boss does."

Some responses to Constant Child Milquetoast bosses may be of disgust, "What a mouse!" Other responses may be quite the opposite. The same boss could be seen by another employee as a "smooth operator" or as someone who "plays fair."

Some responses to Constant Child Milquetoast bosses may be of disgust, "What a mouse!"

Employees tend to see a boss who is a constant Scatterbrain as a young child with a first chemistry set. Such bosses are so inconsistent that they seldom last long as managers. Workers respond to creative Innovators quite differently. One coworkers might say, "I don't always understand the big ideas coming from the think-tank department, but they sure keep things hopping around here." Another might say, "Wow, I wish I could dream up new ideas that easily."

Rightly or wrongly, bosses are seen by others in the plus or minus stereotypes that are a reflection of the three ego states. This may or may not be the way bosses perceive themselves.

Contamination of the Adult

Another common mistake many bosses make is to believe they are thinking clearly when actually their Adult thinking is contaminated.

Contamination occurs when feelings left over from childhood and opinions and prejudices absorbed from parent figures interfere with clear Adult thinking.

Everybody has some contamination, at least in some areas of their lives. Contamination is most frequently experienced when people talk about how to rear children, spend money, engage in sexual intercourse, be politically active. These subjects often arouse strong Childhood feelings and Parental opinions which are *not* based on fact. Contamination is diagramed as:

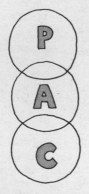

Common Parent contaminations are often expressed as opinions on how a job "should" be run, how training "should" be conducted, the bossing style that "must" be used.

An even more important contamination is that women, or people of a different race, religion, or ethnic background, or older persons, or younger persons, or people who dress or speak in certain ways could not possibly be efficient executives.

If these opinions have not been thought through, they are likely to be expressed as prejudices. Prejudices are strongly held opinions which have not been examined on the basis of objective data.

Common contaminations from the Parent are things such as: men should move the office furniture and carry heavy packages, or women should fix the coffee, bring in the flowers, and make things look pleasant. An even more important contamination is that women, or people of a different race, religion, or ethnic background, or older persons, or younger persons, or people who dress or speak in certain ways could not possibly be efficient executives. Such prejudices are usually based on insufficient evidence.

Contamination of the Adult by the Child ego state shows if feelings of inadequacy lead to overcompliance, or if feelings of anger lead to bullying, or if feelings of conceit lead to show-off behavior.

Many people—subordinates as well as bosses—have Childlike delusions of grandeur that affect their analytical ability. These are delusions concerning their own power or competence or the power or competence of other people. This contamination is expressed in grandiose behavior and words. For example, some subordinates who are without experience may feel "entitled" to the same salary as an experienced person. In their heads, they may exaggerate their competence. This is grandiose. Some bosses may feel "entitled" to make all major decisions. In their heads, they exaggerate the importance of role and title. This is also grandiose and contaminates their clear thinking.

The why of contamination

Contamination often occurs because each ego state in a person may dispose this individual to think and feel differently about a particular issue. For example, a boss who has a target date for a report, but who also wants to take a four-day weekend vacation, is likely to experience some inner conflict with priorities. Inside the boss, the Parent ego state might moralize "work before play," the Child might feel sulky and respond inwardly, "Yes, but I don't want to work," and the Adult might referee with "This project is due Friday."

If unaware of conflicting inner values, this same boss may treat other employees with impatience. The Parent contamination might show in a critical voice; the Child contamination might show in a pleading or whining voice. This contamination would be diagramed as:

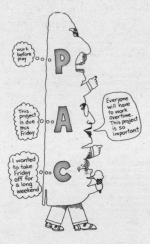

The clearest way to recognize contamination is to consider whether or not objective facts are presented. If not, then communication is likely to be unclear; and the behavior not quite appropriate to the situation. This interferes with effectiveness and efficiency.

If this same boss becomes aware of how punitive the Parental values of "work before pleasure" are, and of the way Childlike desires for a long weekend lead to impatience with others, he or she will become uncontaminated, at least for that moment, and, therefore, a more OK boss.

Self-discovery 2

Energy can shift back and forth from one ego state
to another in people who are not "stuck" in a
particular ego state. When did you last feel or act like
this?

Or like this?

Or like this?

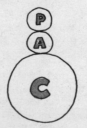

Think of yourself in several recent situations and draw
an ego-state diagram using circles of different sizes to
represent the amount of energy that was seemingly
invested in each state.

How might you draw an ego-state portrait of your
bossing style? Or of your boss's style? Would the size of
the circles change rapidly or not? If so, in what situations?

So what to do

OK bosses make mistakes, but they learn from them. They don't keep making the same ones over and over again.

Are you having trouble with particular employees or coworkers? Stop and think a minute. Are they ill or worried? Did you withhold attention and give them the Shadow treatment when they needed information or encouragement? Were you by any chance a little Scatter-brained or did you crack a joke, act critical, or give a fighting pep-talk that just didn't go over? If so, you probably used the wrong ego state, or the negative side of a bossing stereotype.

You may have missed with a particular person, but you don't need to continue doing so. A basic bit of sage TA advice is, if something isn't working, don't keep hitting your head against a wall. Try something different.

How might you do better next time? One way is to increase your awareness of the individuals with whom you work.

- Pay attention to body language: Are people looking down-cast? Do they have a faraway look and seem to be "not with it?" Do their shoulders droop? Their voices drop? Are they suddenly restless? Unpredict-ably slow, even passive? Do they act as if they're looking for a fight? Or do they appear to be bored and looking for a challenge?

- Pay attention to what they are saying: "I can't do this," "I'm so confused," "I'm doing my best," "It's Max's fault," "I can't go to that meeting right now. I have to call my mother,' "I'm so worried I can hardly work today. My son has a 102° temperature," "I just got engaged!" "If you don't give me that report pretty soon, it will never get typed."

- How do they say it? Are they whining, belligerent, confident, insecure, nervous, excited?

- What ego state do they seem to favor? Under what circumstances do they shift ego states?

Next, based on the information you've gathered, consider your options. First, try another bossing style. For example, if you were to proceed from a Parent ego state and act as an Informed Critic instead of a Critical Dictator, would others "hear" you better? Does the style you've been using interfere with your message? What do your facial expression, tone of voice, gestures, and posture convey? Are they consistent with what you say? Or is a contaminated message coming through?

It's not unusual for someone to vow, "I'm never going to talk to anyone the way my parents talked to me," and then discover themselves doing exactly that.

Other options might include: Apologies, if in order! Counting ten before exploding. Taking time to carefully explain a new program or procedure. Offering encouragement. Giving praise. Cracking a joke. Asking for opinions or information. Arranging an afternoon off work for your employees. Calling a meeting. Setting different priorities.

If you don't like the way others perceive you, what would you have to do differently? Do you need to give more Adult information? More Parental encouragement or critiquing? Do you need to smile more often? What?

Think of a kaleidoscope, the kind children play with. When the cylinder is turned, bits of broken glass at one end form a new pattern. You can use any of your ego states in conjunction with your Adult by turning around and using more of your total self.

Effective and efficient personalities

At any time or place the use of one ego state over another may be more effective. Some employees seem to work best with a Parental-type boss. Others respond more positively to a thoughtful Adult-type boss. Still others prefer the boss who shows a lot of Childlike behavior.

Effective and efficient OK bosses know that flexibility is an important key to success. They do the right thing by shifting energy from one ego state to another, when shifts are appropriate. This is being both effective and efficient.

Even as each stereotype has a positive side, so too has each ego state. Each can be used in OK ways.

It is appropriate to use some nurturing Parent if someone is injured or grieving, or some critical Parent if someone is goofing up, or some more liberating Parent if someone is already performing well.

It's appropriate to use some fighting Partner tactics in going for a contract. Or to use some fair Negotiating skills to wrap up an important contract. Or to use some fun-loving Child expressions in celebrating a new contract.

It's also appropriate to use the Adult-as-Executive to decide when, where, how, and with whom to use the other parts of the personality.

This capacity to become aware of the needs and interests of others and to appropriately shift ego states or bossing styles to maximize their potentials increases everyone's OKness.

3

Psychological positions and OK bosses

OK and not-OK attitudes

All bosses have some measure of control over others. They have assigned and often assumed responsibility. They may function in a highly structured way or informally.

The bossing may be exhibited positively as critiquing, supporting, or noninterfering Parental behavior. Or as responsive, analytical Adult behavior. Or as cooperative, negotiating, creative Childlike behavior.

Bossing may also be exhibited negatively as opinionated, or overnurturing, or indifferent Parental behavior. Or as mechanistic Adult behavior. Or as hostile, or apologetic, or scatterbrained Childlike behavior.

Transactions with others reflect how bosses feel about themselves as being OK or not-OK. They also reflect how they feel about others as being OK or not-OK.

In transactional analysis the feelings of OKness and not-OKness are called *psychological positions*. They are generalized attitudes about people in general.

1. I (we) are OK, you (they) are OK.

2. I (we) are OK, you (they) are not-OK.

3. I (we) are not-OK, you (they) are OK.

4. I (we) are not-OK, you (they) are not-OK.

People in the first position of I'm OK, You're OK feel basically *Confident* and constructive. This is a "get along with" people position.

People in the second position of I'm OK, You're not-OK tend to act *Superior* and arrogant. This is a "get rid of" people position because their style drives people away.

People in the third position of I'm not-OK, You're OK feel basically *Depressed* and inferior. This is a "get away from" people position as such people tend to withdraw from others and feel discouraged about themselves.

People in the fourth position of I'm not-OK, You're not-OK feel basically *Hopeless* and futile. This is a "get nowhere with" people position because such people give up easily.

OK and not-OK psychological positions

Psychological positions are easily spotted in many home and work situations. They show in gestures, facial expressions, posture, and other forms of body language. An affectionate grin conveys a message of "I like you and I like me." A frown or sneer conveys quite the opposite.

The tone of voice can often be a tip-off. Imagine how four different bosses might speak to an employee regarding a job description:

Confident boss—I'm OK, You're OK
"Your job description is going to be changed somewhat. I'd like you to be satisfied with the changes before they are finally decided."

Superiority boss—I'm OK, You're not-OK
"Your job description has been changed while you were on vacation. You'll need to abide by the new description."

Depressed boss—I'm not-OK, You are OK
"Your job description has been changed, but I'm not quite sure about it. You've been here longer than I have, so you might have better ideas about it."

Hopeless boss—I'm not-OK, You're not-OK
"Your job has been changed. The changes aren't much good, but it probably won't matter anyway."

According to the bossing style that is being used, the OK or not-OK positions will be expressed differently.

For instance, the Loner boss, speaking from an I'm OK, You're not-OK position, may say, "I don't have much time right now, but your job has been changed somewhat. John will tell you more about it."

The mechanistic Computer boss, from the same psycho-logical position, might say, "Since we already have five writers, each of whom can produce three advertisements a day, I am going to change your job from writer to coordinator of the agency newsletter."

The Confident, Superior, Depressed, and Hopeless bosses may often say the same thing, "Your job descrip-tion is going to be changed somewhat. I'd like you to be satisfied with the changes before they are finally decided," but their tone of voice and their body language may convey quite a different message:

The Confident boss conveys the idea, "I respect you and will consider your ideas." (I'm OK, You're OK).

The Superiority boss conveys the idea, "I'm the boss, and you'll have to take the description whether you like it or not." (I'm OK, You're not-OK).

The Depressed boss conveys the idea, "I'm not adequate as I haven't written the description clearly, but you'll naturally understand anyway." (I'm not-OK, You are OK).

The Hopeless boss conveys the idea, "Nothing is any good, including the job description, and it wouldn't matter if it were." (I'm not-OK, You're not-OK).

Hiring practices of OK and not-OK bosses

Psychological positions can be observed in any area of responsibility, including *hiring practices*. For example:

Confident bosses tend to seek out confident employees and encourage anxious and depressed employees to develop their fullest potential. They are not upset by the occasional person who acts superior, and are able to delegate authority when it is appropriate.

Superiority bosses usually seek out anxious or depressed employees and aim to keep them there. Occasionally

they get employees who fight against being in a lower position. These employees may act even more superior than their boss and may threaten to gain control in one way or another. Frequently, the Superiority boss tries to "keep down those rebellious upstarts."

Depressed bosses feel inadequate. They often attract those who act superior or arrogant, willing to tell the boss what to do. If they hire either confident or depressed employees, they often become more depressed by negatively comparing themselves to the confident ones or by identifying with the others who are also depressed.

Hopeless bosses are those who've given up and "thrown in the sponge." If they have confident or superiority-type employees, they feel even more hopeless and futile. If they have either depressed or hopeless employees, they feel locked into their position.

Facilities, equipment, and OK bosses

Psychological positions are also reflected in the physical facilities and equipment that are supplied to employees. Although some bosses do not have budget control and are therefore unable to facilitate any kind of change, others do.

Confident bosses seek to provide a comfortable environment for their employees, as well as for themselves, with good ventilation and temperature control. The working situation is clean, often attractive. The furniture fits the bodies of those using it. The acoustics are planned so that neither bosses nor subordinates are fatigued by a constant barrage of noise. Lighting is given careful attention and the lounge areas show warmth and creativity in their decor.

Superiority bosses are more concerned over their own comfort, and sometimes the comfort of their customers, than that of their own employees. They may easily rationalize the acquisition of new furniture for themselves without awareness that their subordinates' furniture may be out of date, impractical, or downright uncomfortable. Some Superiority bosses order large quantities of matching furniture at discount. Whereas the furniture may match and be aesthetically pleasing to the eye, it may not be compatible with the personalities or bodies of those who use it. Superiority bosses may not be interested in other people's comfort or working situation unless it can be exploited.

Depressed bosses are often those who work in dingy holes and give the "best" to others—other bosses, subordinates, or customers. They negatively compare themselves with those whom they see as being more OK than they are. They may not care if their department also works in substandard, or unattractive, or inefficient surroundings. The secretaries may have to "make do" with poor equipment, the supervisors may be denied a training budget, those with responsibility may have no power to implement it, and so forth. This happens when Depressed bosses exhibit the psychological position of I or my department is not-OK.

Hopeless bosses, having given up, do nothing. After all, they believe that they are not OK and neither are their subordinates, so why try? They believe that neither their firm nor any other similar firm is OK, so it really does not matter what the physical conditions are. At one time they were probably Depressed bosses who placed some value on others; then they gave up—even on others.

Employee psychological positions

Employees, having needs, skills, and feelings, naturally respond in ways that reflect their own psychological positions. They too may be confident, taking an I'm OK, You're OK position. They may also express one of the other positions.

Possible responses to being given a new job description might be:

Confident employee—I'm OK, You're OK
"Thanks for asking about what I think. I do have some ideas I think might be useful to both of us."

Superiority employee—I'm OK, You're not-OK
"That job description won't do at all, and the union will back me up in my position. Evidently, you haven't reviewed the contract."

Depressed employee—I'm not-OK, You're OK
"Thank you very much for the job description. I'm sure whatever you decided will be OK with me, but I don't know if I can do it."

Hopeless employee—I'm not-OK, You're not-OK
"Yeah, OK. I'll try. But it won't work anyhow."

Like bosses, any employee's response may be a strong, "up front" one or more subtle. The tendency is to be more subtle when approaching a boss. The person packing merchandise is likely to be "careful" when approaching a supervisor. The supervisors may be "careful" when approaching a manager. Similarly, the manager may be cautious when going to a top executive, and the executive may be cautious with a board of directors.

Psychological positions at home

The four psychological positions are often apparent at home as well as at work. Consider a mother asking her teenage son to clean up his room.

Confident boss: Last week you and I agreed that your room would be clean by tonight. What can we do to keep that agreement?

Superiority boss: Your room is always a mess and so are you. You'd better get upstairs and clean your room before I tell your father. I don't know where you learned to be so messy. Certainly not from me!

Depressed boss: Your room is a mess. But I guess that you know better than I how you like to live.

Hopeless boss: Your room is always a mess and so are you. I want you to clean it up right now. But, what the hell, you never listen to me anyway.

Multiple bosses at work and at home

Whether a boss carries a label of director, executive manager, teacher, supervisor, or mother, most have some managing responsibility to get the job done and get it done through people.

Your room is always
a mess and so are you.
You'd better get upstairs
and clean your room
before I tell your father.
I don't know where you
learned to be so messy.
Certainly not from me!

The most OK firms are those that have Confident I'm OK, You're OK bosses on every level of management. The least OK are those firms where the bosses feel hopeless, or not-OK about themselves and not-OK about others.

Some bosses are responsible for hiring; other bosses may be responsible for training, or for planning and organizing, or for directing and appraising performance, and so forth. Each may choose certain types of employees, those whose personalities fit theirs. What may please one boss may not please another.

For the employee who has several bosses, each using a different positive or negative bossing style, this may be difficult. Furthermore, each may transact from a different psychological position.

If one boss is "heavier" than the other, the employee needs special skill in handling each of them. When this is the case, he or she may feel like a juggler trying to keep all the oranges up in the air at once, or like a magician who needs to pull rabbits out of hats.

As in business, the most successful families have Confident I'm OK, You're OK bosses on every level of management. But families have bossing situations somewhat different than businesses—it is frequently hard to discover who is "the boss" in a family because roles and responsibilities usually are not as clearly defined as in business.

The teenage son who is asked to clean up his room is often at a far greater disadvantage than his father's or mother's employees. First of all, he usually has at least two bosses whose perceptions, ideas, and authority sometimes conflict.

His mother may want him to clean his room, but his father may say, "Ah, let him read his comics. He can clean the room later."

If the son has older brothers and sisters, he may have to
adjust to even more bosses. In addition, he may also
be a boss of a younger brother and sister (or the dog)
and he too needs to learn how to successfully manage
others. Like a subordinate, he also feels like a juggler,
trying to keep everyone (including himself!) happy.
Juggling skills become important because, unlike an
employee, the teenage son cannot quit or get transferred
to another division.

Self-discovery 3

Most bosses experience all of the four psychological positions from time to time. Some days they feel right and OK; other days they feel just the opposite. It's not surprising.

Think of a recent problem in your work or at home. What psychological positions did you take?

■ I'm OK, You're OK _____

■ I'm OK, You're not-OK _____

■ I'm not-OK, You're OK _____

■ I'm not-OK, You're not-OK _____

What position did other people *think* you took?

What positions did they take?

What would have happened if each person had responded from the I'm OK, You're OK position?

What would each person have said?

Using your Adult, figure out why you or others didn't respond from a Confident position.

Which psychological position do you favor at work? At home?

How about your subordinates, your coworkers, your boss, your spouse?

So what to do

When you think about your boss or bosses, what feeling do you usually have? Is it a "gut" feeling of anger or depression, appreciation and liking, or what?

If you feel not-OK, then have a brainstorming session with yourself to develop a list of possible things you might do.

Maybe you need to take a more positive Parental role with your boss. Maybe you need to learn how to crack a joke once in a while. Or talk less. Or "come up fighting" more often. Or go off on your own creative tangent.

As a boss yourself, there are many things you can do to convey a double-OK position. "Smile and the world smiles with you; cry and you cry alone" is an old cliche that still has lots of merit. Let other people know you think they're OK, and they will probably respond positively.

Look around your working situation. If it's drab, then brighten it up. If it's uncomfortable, make it comfortable, even if you have to spend some of your own money. So what! You're worth it, aren't you?

Look around where others work. Is there anything that needs to be done that you might do? Want to do? Have the power to do? If so, don't hold back. Use all the "clout" you're got to upgrade not-OKness to OK.

Effective and efficient psychological positions

There are times when some people need to be criticized, need to have limits set, need to have demands made upon them. Not everyone is a self-starter. Confident bosses get others going while still conveying an I'm OK and so are you message.

There are also times when some people need to be encouraged, nurtured, cared for, and forgiven. Many people do not receive enough of this kind of help.

Confident bosses recognize it and put out the extra effort without conveying a You're not-OK attitude.

There are times when some people need to be left alone, need to be given freedom to do some independent thinking. Some people have overcritical or overnurturing bosses, when instead they need Shadow bosses and some distance to be effective. Confident bosses, generally feeling OK, are willing to share the feeling by giving others some space in which to grow.

Occasionally, people need to be encouraged to fight for what they want. Or they may need to be pacified so that they stop fighting when it's not productive. Or they may need to be stimulated to get on with their creative OKness. Confident bosses allow this to happen.

Effective bosses know that OK constructive criticism and OK emotional support may both be necessary. They also know efficiency increases in a Confident I'm OK, You're OK atmosphere. They do everything possible to bring it about.

They tune in to nonverbal messages from their subordinates. They hear the nonverbal messages from their bosses. They become aware of their own nonverbal messages that they give out. They change—at least in themselves—what needs to be changed. Then they discover that changing themselves for the better often elicits positive change in others.

4

Bosses
who stroke
and
bosses
who don't

OK and not-OK strokes

The word *stroke* is a colloquial TA term. It refers to any form of recognition—a word such as "Hello," a gesture such as a handshake.

Strokes can be verbal or nonverbal, positive or negative. A warm smile or a pat on the back are positive nonverbal strokes. A frown or an abrupt turning away are negative nonverbal strokes.

Greeting a person and using his or her name, "Hi, Joe," "Good morning, Ann," or giving an honest compliment are positive verbal strokes. Growling in response to a question or greeting someone sarcastically with, "Well, at last you've arrived!" are negative verbal strokes.

All people need strokes. If they can't get positive ones, then they will take negative ones. To many people, negative strokes are better than no strokes at all.

Conditional and unconditional strokes

All strokes are also either unconditional or conditional. *Unconditional strokes* are words or behavior that convey the message, "I like you just because you're you, not for what you achieve." The unconditional stroke is the kind all infants need. It helps them develop a basic I'm OK position.

Unconditional strokes are seldom given on the job unless those involved are basically friendly towards each other as well as being coworkers. Unconditional strokes off the job may also be scarce between spouses or friends. Yet everybody needs them and needs to figure out ways to get them.

Conditional strokes are words or some kind of body language that convey, "I approve of you if you . . . (agree with me, placate me, obey me, work hard for me, etc.)." Conditional strokes are the kind most commonly given by all kinds of bosses.

Conditional strokes are words or some kind of body language that convey, "I approve of you if you placate me"

Bossing styles and stroking patterns

Each bossing style and each OK or not-OK position can be observed in the stroking patterns bosses use.

From their OK side, *Informed Critics* often expect excellence. They usually stroke employees conditionally until excellence does occur. They might say, "You can do it if you put a little more effort into it," or "This report will be fine if you work it over one more time." These kinds of conditional strokes may contain a message of "I'm OK and You're OK if you work towards perfection." They are often efficient forms of recognition.

Critical Dictators, operating from the not-OK Critic side, frequently give negative verbal strokes. They may yell or make sarcastic remarks such as, "What's the matter, can't you do anything right!" Or they may imply the same thing nonverbally by frowning, sneering or pounding on the desk. Their stroking pattern carries a message of "I'm OK, You'll Never Be OK unless you buckle down and do things my way."

Supportive Coaches, from their positive OK side, may encourage those who act inadequate, confused, or helpless to become more competent. They give strokes of emotional support. They help others only until they become self-supporting. They give out a message, usually nonverbal, "I'm OK *and* I'm willing to work with you," and "You're OK if you're willing to learn how to do it."

Benevolent Dictators, from their not-OK side, tend to give phony, even syrupy, strokes like, "I know you can do it if you don't worry about it," "You'll get it done if you let me help you." They project a subtle message of "I'm OK and I can rescue you, You're not-OK (stay helpless)." Their stroking patterns give recognition to subordinates who act confused or inadequate. After all, Coaches, from their not-OK side, need inadequate people so they will have someone to nurture.

Liberators, the OK flip side of Shadow bosses, tend to stroke only in rare situations. But their strokes may be particularly effective and appreciated because they are so rare. Furthermore, subordinates of these kinds of Shadow bosses may learn, out of sheer desperation, to compliment themselves or to seek out strokes from other significant persons. People who do not need a boss as a parent substitute work well when left alone.

Loner bosses often try to hide their own feelings of not-OKness. They seldom look for strokes from others and do not acknowledge the need other people have for words and gestures of recognition. Consequently, the strokes they do give are often minimal, with little substance. Actually, the Loner's indifference sometimes masks hopelessness: "I don't get any recognition, so why should I give it to anyone else?" Frozen out themselves, they often freeze out others. Yet to be ignored is painful—it is like solitary confinement.

Communicators, from their positive analytical side, often smile and speak briefly to any coworker they contact in the hall, parking lot, water cooler, and so forth. They listen well. They respond to the nonverbal as well as the verbal statements of their subordinates and bosses. If they discover a high turnover of personnel and low productivity of goods, they may conclude the working conditions are emotionally sterile and their employees are stroke-hungry. If so, such bosses may then choose to act even more friendly and spend more time stroking others.

Computer bosses, from their not-OK side, may also give few strokes. They may seldom stop by a desk to compliment someone on their appearance, or inquire about a person's health, or ask how things are at home. Their statements and questions are usually computed around economic values. They give conditional strokes, often nonverbally implying "You're OK if you think clearly, if you stay within the budget, and if you always perform rationally."

Partners are OK people who fight fairly. They may stir up the juices of competition in others. Their challenging ways often elicit strong team support. They "go, go, go." They "get in there and pitch." They often fight for their subordinates, for their peers, and even for their bosses. They also give strokes to others who act like Partners.

Punk bosses, with their emphasis on competitiveness, seem to give out a lot of negative strokes. They may slap a person hard on the back while making a sarcastic statement such as, "Let's see if *you* can match that quota," or "Hey, you sure will have to work to win the prize for the best performance this month." Such bosses give out messages of "I'm OK, but You're not-OK if you won't fight."

Negotiators are OK Pacifiers because of their lack of hostility. They intuit people's feelings and tend to give the kinds of strokes that are expected. They avoid conflict with remarks such as, "Let's see if we can all get along better," or "That doesn't seem worth fighting about." They use pleasant "hellos," and clearly give out strokes that convey the message of "I'm OK, You're OK; let's solve the problem without a big fight."

Milquetoast bosses often give out bland, blah strokes. They seldom show excitement or enthusiasm. Even if a sales person is very successful, a Milquetoast boss may act nervous and say, "Fine, but don't talk about it or others on the staff might get jealous."

Innovative inventor bosses may be very effective. They may give approving Parental strokes to others who are also creative. They may recognize employees with an exciting party, retirement gift, or a fresh kind of staff-training program. The strokes they give others may also come from their Child ego state and may be directed to the other person's Child ego state. Statements such as, "Wow, great idea," or "Fantastic, wish I'd thought of that," are typical. This encourages further creativity, and most people enjoy receiving these kinds of strokes.

From the not-OK pole, Scatterbrain bosses may get so wrapped up in their own experiments that they ignore others and forget to stroke them.

when they do this, their psychological position is, "I'm OK, I'm so energy-filled or charismatic, you're not-OK unless you stroke me for my terrific ideas"

From the not-OK pole, inventors are Scatterbrained bosses who may get so wrapped up in their own experiments that they ignore others and forget to stroke them. When they do this, their psychological position is, "I'm OK, I'm so energy-filled or charismatic; You're not-OK unless you stroke me for my terrific ideas."

Target strokes for different folks

A target stroke is a very specific stroke. It is designed for a particular person, given for a particular reason. It is carefully thought out and carefully executed. It can be OK or not-OK.

OK target strokes, either verbal or nonverbal, conditional or unconditional, are designed to enhance others. They can be given from any ego state and sent to any ego state. They are positive strokes that really "hit the target." They are what the other person hopes to hear.

Target strokes can be simple, unconditional messages such as a look that says, "I'm glad you're you," or a sudden, "Hey, let's go to lunch together," or a sincere, "I'm glad you work here."

Target strokes can also be conditional recognition of performance. Employees often look for these kinds of strokes.

Currently, more and more women on the job are asking for strokes that recognize the rational thinking of their Adult. This is instead of, or in addition to, the strokes they get for their nurturing Parent that may make the coffee, and their fun-loving Child that may joke around.

In contrast, many men are looking for the kind of strokes that historically women have received in abundance. Men also have nurturing qualities; they want strokes for Parenting skill. Men also are fun-loving, and some also want the Child in them to be recognized. The liberated man tends to believe that "all work and no play makes Jack a dull man."

Yet each person's stroke needs are different. Take the problem of absenteeism, for example. One employee may want a stroke for Adult rational thinking and may get it when the manager says, "I'm glad you gave me those figures on absenteeism for your department. Now I understand some of your supervisory problems more clearly."

Some employees want Parental strokes of approval instead of straight Adult feedback. They might get it with responses such as, "I appreciate your working overtime to give me those figures on absenteeism. You really do have a supervisory problem, but I can see you're trying hard."

Others may wish for a stroke that comes from the boss's Child and is directed to their Child ego state. They may get it with a comment such as, "Wow, those absentee figures show you have a really tough supervisory problem. You'll just have to 'hang in there,' and it ain't going to be easy."

In any one person, each of the three ego states may want different strokes. Tom, Dick, and Sherry are examples:

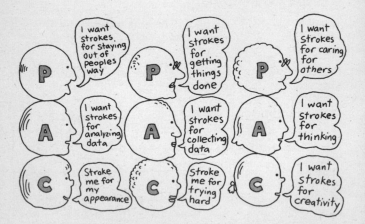

Tom   Dick   Sherry

Some people are aware of their stroke needs, some are not. People's stroke needs change from time to time. What they want one day may not be the same as what they want the day after.

Not-OK target strokes

Not-OK target strokes are verbal or nonverbal strokes that are designed to hurt someone else, to make someone feel inadequate in some way.

A look of disapproval or a remark such as, "You look terrible the way you're dressed today," may really hurt someone who has a low self-esteem about appearance.

A sneer or a remark such as, "You couldn't sell anything important if you tried," is likely to alienate people who already doubt their sales abilities and discourage them from learning how to be successful.

Some jokes are thin veils for not-OK target strokes. Ridicule or sarcasm are the same, though more direct. Any kind of barb which is given from an I'm OK, You're not-OK position usually reflects the sometimes crude, often hostile, not-OKness of the stroker. This includes comments such as "That's a pretty good presentation— for a woman!" or "Not bad—for a kid like you!"

Such remarks can be aimed at a target in such a way that they eventually backfire, and those who make such remarks may begin to wonder why people avoid them. "After all," the joker may say, "I'm just trying to be friendly. What's the matter with everyone? Can't they take a joke!"

Self-discovery 4

Select five people to think about that you interacted with during the past week. Recall the strokes you gave them:

- Were the strokes conditional or unconditional?

- From which of your ego states did they come?

- To what ego state in the other person did they go?

- Did they hit the target?

Recall the strokes you received this week:

- What kind were they?

- Did they hit the target in you as not-OK, "cold pricklies" or as OK "warm fuzzies?"

Now think about the strokes you gave and the strokes you got:

- Are there any changes that would increase your OKness or the OKness of others?

So what to do

Regardless of the bossing style a person has been using, regardless of the not-OK psychological positions a boss has been showing, change can happen.

Bosses who become aware of their own negative stereotype, their own negative psychological positions, and the effect of negatives on other employees can choose to be different. This may include you.

- You can choose to operate from your own positive pole rather than your negative pole.

- You can choose to transact with others from the psychological position of a winner, which is I'm OK, You're OK.

- You can choose to give a few unconditional, as well as conditional, strokes to others.

- You can choose to give strokes to others that hit the target.

There are several ways to discover the target. One is to simply ask a question such as, "What would you like to hear from me?" If the response indicates that the employee does not know the answer, then carefully observe what seems to turn that person on, what kind of action or remark from you adds bounce to their walk, lights up their face or eyes, or results in a renewed enthusiasm for the job.

Another way to discover the target is with the use of imagination, intuition, and two chairs. This method would not be appropriate in a busy work situation. It needs to be experimented with when you're alone. You may feel a little silly or strange when you first try it. Don't let that hold you back. Stick with it.

The method is to sit in one chair. Imagine the other person in a chair close by and facing you. Start a dialogue. Say what you want to say. Then switch chairs and be that other person responding positively or negatively to your stroke. Continue the dialogue while switching chairs back and forth until the transaction feels completed.

Bosses need strokes too

Naturally, a boss also needs strokes. Sometimes all they get are "cold pricklies" when what they need are "warm fuzzies."

How about you? Do you want strokes? From your boss? Your peers? Your subordinates? What kind do you want? Conditional strokes for what you do? Or unconditional ones for who you are?

Look in your mirror and talk to yourself. Ask yourself what you want and need. Try the double chairs. Put yourself in one and imagine your boss, or peer, or subordinate in the other. Start the dialogue to bring your stroke needs into awareness.

As another way, go back in your memory bank where your childhood experiences are stored. Recall once more some of the target strokes you got then, or wanted to get. These actual or wish-for strokes are what you may still be wanting.

If you feel uncomfortable asking someone for strokes, then spend some time thinking about the question, "What's the worst thing that could happen if I ask for what I want?" The answer may surprise you!

A basic TA premise is that people are basically OK and will respond that way if their stroking needs are met. However, many things happen to people so that they may stop feeling and acting positively. They begin to act not-OK. This is because they carry a lot of "garbage" around with them; garbage comes from negative stroking in the past. It's important to get rid of the garbage. The OK boss will recognize a person's garbage as only that— garbage—and will know and act as though underneath it all is an OK person.

Effective and efficient stroking

Some bosses, when acting not-OK, may spray strokes around hoping that some will land on fertile soil. Strokes that are sprayed around are seldom effective or efficient. Bosses, from their OK side, will think about how their strokes might be focused and on target rather than sprayed and off target.

They know that everyone needs strokes. Some people need more strokes of a certain kind than others. Without these particular strokes, they tend to shrivel up in some way.

Their work may go sour, their ideas may become less creative, they may be absent more often, and their errors and poor decisions may increase. Though competent, they may quit in favor of an organization that gives positive strokes more generously.

An OK boss will learn what kinds of strokes will hit the target. He or she will be willing to give them so that other people may also feel more OK.

OK bosses will also figure out what strokes they need for themselves and what they need to do to get them.

5

Transactional
bossing

Types of transactions

In TA terms, the things that people do and say to each other are called *transactions*. In a transaction, each person gains something from the exchange. What they give and what they get depends upon which ego state in each person is most active at the time and the kinds of transactions that go on between them.

There are three types of transactions—complementary, crossed, and ulterior. Any one of these transactions, whether between bosses, or between a boss and a subordinate, is sometimes OK, sometimes not-OK. It depends on what the goal of the transaction is. One goal might be to offer encouragement, another might be to render criticism, still another might be to gain information.

In every transaction, there is at least one *stimulus*, which is a stroke of some kind, and one *response*, which is also a stroke. "Hi, Harriet," is a positive stimulus stroke. "Hi, Bill, how are you?" is a positive response stroke.

This kind of everyday greeting is called a *complementary transaction* because the stimulus receives the expected response. Another kind of complementary transaction would be a bossy boss, speaking to a Childlike employee and getting a Childlike response. Or a Fighting boss, speaking to a feisty employee and getting a feisty response. Complementary transactions may or may not be compliments.

If the response to a stimulus is not an expected one, the transaction is said to be *crossed*. This occurs if the greeting "Hi, Harriet" gets a critical response such as, "Don't you see I'm busy?" or a plaintive response such as, "Please don't ask me how I am." With such responses, Bill is likely to feel crossed up somehow.

The third type of transaction is *ulterior*. It is called this because an ostensible Adult-to-Adult stimulus partially hides a different message that is directed to the Child ego state in the other person. A "Hi, Harriet" given with a wink or a sneer is this kind of ulterior transaction. The ulterior message is usually given by body language or tone of voice.

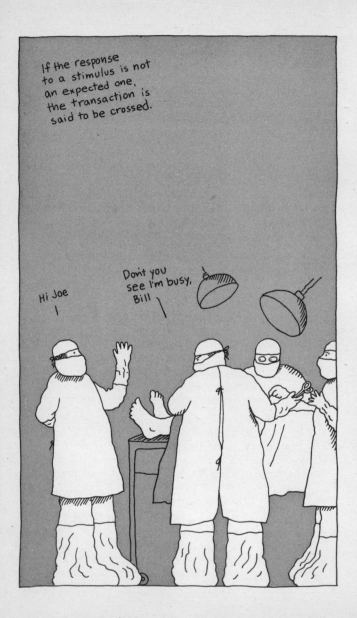

OK and not-OK complementary transactions

Complementary transactions, which occur when a person gets his or her expected response, can occur between any two ego states. Complementary transactions are diagramed with parallel lines:

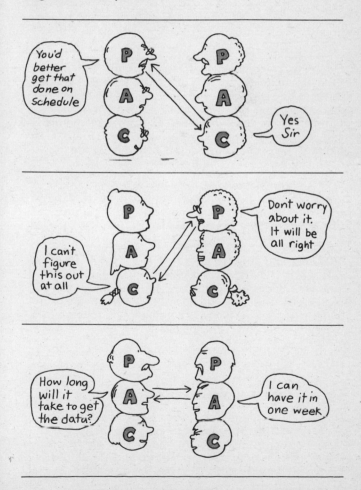

Of course, complementary transactions may be initiated from an employee, as well as from a boss. For example, an employee may speak with a whine or look downcast and expect, and get, a Parental response. Or an employee may present a draft for a new program and expect, and get, clear Adult feedback. In either case, if the lines between ego states are parallel, communication is open and can continue indefinitely.

Constant complementary transactions are not always good, however. If two people continually have Parent-to-Child complementary transactions, as in the first diagram, then they can become locked into specific roles.

This pattern retards the growth of the person who is overusing and abusing the Child ego state and saying things like, "I don't make decisions. I only work here." The same pattern may frustrate the other person, who is likely to be overusing and abusing the Parent ego state and saying, "I'll decide what's going to be done and no one else. And don't you forget it!"

Frequent transactions such as the above are not-OK.

OK and not-OK crossed transactions

Crossed transactions occur when the expected response is not given. The lines between ego states cross and communication breaks down. The person who is crossed often feels misunderstood, or surprised and confused. Common crossed transactions may be diagrammed as:

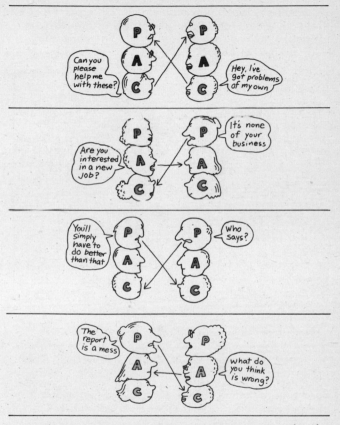

Crossed transactions are sometimes OK. For example, if a customer or coworker talks on and on indefinitely, an OK cross might be, "Yes, you've told me that," or "I feel uncomfortable when you reexplain." Another cross might be to change the subject.

If someone speaks in a confused manner, using generalities or unclear terminology, an OK cross might be, "Is there something you'd like to say but haven't quite formulated?" or "I think it would speed up our decision if you outline your proposal first."

If someone is avoiding a problem, an OK cross might be, "Let's set a time for talking this problem through," or "Is this something that you see as needing correction, or shall we just let it go?"

Bosses, from their not-OK side, often use crossed transactions in such a way that others feel put-down, misunderstood, and not-OK. When this occurs, morale, production, and services are likely to drop.

Bosses, from their OK sides, use crossed transactions as management tools to help themselves and others to work more efficiently.

OK and not-OK ulterior transactions

Ulterior transactions are those that have a hidden agenda. They are more complex than complementary and crossed transactions as they involve more than two ego states at once.

An ulterior message is often given nonverbally by *body language*. An employee may, for example, angrily pound a desk, turn away abruptly, or give an encouraging pat on the shoulder. An ulterior message may also be given by the facial expression. An employee may wink seductively, laugh joyfully, or frown disapprovingly.

An ulterior transaction may also be given with a *tone of voice*. An employee who plaintively whines, sarcastically ridicules, or looks helplessly confused conveys a powerful message.

An ulterior transaction may also be given with a tone of voice. An employee who plaintively whines, sarcastically ridicules, or looks helplessly confused conveys a powerful message.

It is the intuitive ability, which everyone has in his or her Child ego state, that is used to pick up ulterior messages. The creative ability, also present in every Child ego state, is what is used to send out ulterior messages.

The actual words that are spoken are called the *social* transaction. They are diagramed with a solid line. The ulterior message is the psychological transaction. It is diagramed with a dotted line. Common ulterior transactions are:

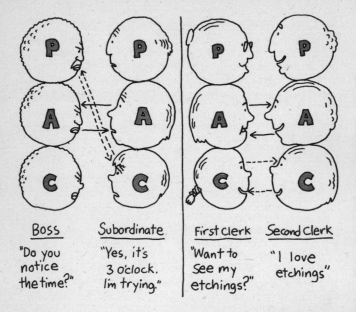

Boss	Subordinate	First Clerk	Second Clerk
"Do you notice the time?"	"Yes, it's 3 o'clock. I'm trying."	"Want to see my etchings?"	"I love etchings"

At the social level, the Adult ego state in the above transactions seems to be doing the talking. Actually, it is one of the other ego states that is sending the "psychological" message.

Sometimes it's more effective to send an ulterior message. A frown may work better than a bawling-out. A depressed expression may work better than a direct, "Can I take off early?" Pacing the floor may be more effective than "Damn it, can't you ever hurry up?"

Discount transactions

In TA, a *discount* is the lack of attention or the negative attention that hurts someone physically or emotionally. Any kind of transaction may include a discount of one (or both) of the people involved.

Sarcasm is a frequent on-the-job discount of someone else. It carries the message, "You're not-OK, you're stupid." Complaining is another frequent discount. It is a discount of oneself, and carries the message "I'm not OK, I'm helpless."

When bosses discount, they ignore or deny the feelings, thoughts, or opinions of themselves or others. They may defensively refuse to examine alternatives and suggest something like, "I've made up my mind, so don't confuse me with the facts." They may question the judgment of others with hostility, "What makes you think you're right?" They may discredit the importance of a problem or of another person's self-esteem.

Many discount transactions are related to problem solving. There are four ways this may be done.

The first way is to discount the *problem itself*. Some bosses ignore obvious departmental dissatisfaction which is reflected in lower productivity and increasing personnel turnover. Or they may ignore symptoms such as alcoholism, depression, or confusion in their employees. Unknowingly, Critical Dictators and Computers discount their own problems. They discount their own bodily or emotional needs for rest and recreation, and often drive themselves until they collapse.

The second type of discount is a denial of the *significance* of the problem. An example of this is when bosses are aware of driving themselves but don't do anything about it. They may agree, "Yes, I'm overly tired, but it's not that important. I'll bounce back." Or they may recognize symptoms in others and again discount the significance of the symptoms. Loners, Milquetoasts, and Scatterbrains are especially prone to discounting in this way.

The third type of discount is to deny that there is a *solution* to the problem. This discount is often used by a Benevolent Dictator who tries to cheer people up while telling them, "You'll just have to live with the problem. There's nothing that can be done." These bosses speak this way to their own inner Child as well as to their employees.

The fourth kind of discount is the denial of *personal ability* to solve a problem. The Punk boss may say, "No matter how hard I fight, there's nothing *I* can do." The Scatterbrain may say something like, "I can't do anything to get people to understand me." The Critical Dictator may affirm, "I can't do a thing with those S.O.B.'s." And so on.

Any type of boss from his or her not-OK side may discount in each of the four ways. OK bosses do not.

They do not ignore or exaggerate the importance of problems, nor do they deny the significance and solubility of them. People's opinions, the feelings they experience, the rational thinking they are capable of, are as important to the OK boss as is getting the product out on time.

Self-discovery 5

Think back on transactions you've had in the last 24 hours.

- Jot down two complementary transactions that you experienced. Were they OK or not-OK?

- Jot down two crossed transactions that you experienced. Were they OK or not-OK?

- Jot down two ulterior transactions that you experienced. Were they OK or not-OK?

- Jot down any discounts that came from these transactions.

Think of three people with whom you are closely associated. What are the most common ways you transact with each of the three?

Are the transactions satisfying? If not, what might you do differently?

Are your transactions full of discounts? If so, write them down. Then reconstruct the conversation without any discounts. Practice saying sentences that are straight and contain no discounts.

So what to do

Changing a style of transacting is not always easy.
Familiar ways of bossing often seem "right" to the person
who is using those ways. Furthermore, other employees
may have become "accustomed" to Joe "just the way
he is" or to Mary "always acting that way." If Joe or
Mary do something different, some employees may feel
confused or hostile.

So what to do? One thing is to admit that maybe your
transactions are not always OK. Sure, you probably do
fine when things are going well. For most people, it's
harder when the pressure's on. You may need to mend
some fences and apologize to someone, or you may
need to listen longer to someone before responding.
Or you may need to assert yourself more.

Look at the morale around work. Is it high or low? Is
motivation high or low? Is performance high or low?
Is turnover high or low?

Be gutsy. Diagram some of your recent transactions with
others. Do they contain discounts? If they follow a
pattern and things aren't going right, what might you
do differently?

Look at your recent letters or interoffice memos. The
stimulus you gave out came from which of your ego
states? To which ego state was your letter or memo
directed? If you didn't get your expected response,
why not?

Now consider the responses you made to other people's
letters or memos. What ego states were involved?
Did you give the expected response? Why or why not?

Become aware of the transactions you use most often
at work and at home.

Are they effective, or are they merely comfortable? Do
they include discounts? If you're not satisfied with your
transactions, decide how to change them, then do it!

This time try holding up a magnifying mirror to yourself. Be aware of the transactions you use most often.

Transactions of effective and efficient bosses

The way all bosses transact often reflects the positive and negative poles of their bossing style, the favorite ego states they use, and the psychological positions they have taken.

OK bosses recognize the value of clear, direct communication and, whenever possible, use complementary transactions. Sometimes they deliberately cross a transaction. Sometimes they use ulterior messages to get their point across when a more open statement might not be acceptable to the other person. They avoid discounting themselves and others.

Complementary, crossed, and ulterior transactions each have values. Communication can be closed off if appropriate. It can be opened up if it needs to be. It can become authentic if it's been phony. It can be OK if not-OK.

Knowing the value of good communication is one of the signs of an effective boss. Knowing how to use each kind of transaction when desirable is one of the signs of an efficient boss. OK bosses continually upgrade their effectiveness and efficiency.

6

Games bosses play

Games defined

Everyone plays psychological games. From the lowest person on the totem pole to the board of directors, everyone initiates his or her own game or gets "hooked" into playing someone else's games.

People are seldom aware they are into a game until the game is over. Then they feel not-OK in some way; or they feel self-righteous, and the other person who has been playing is likely to feel bad.

In TA theory, a game is defined as a series of complementary transactions which seem OK on the surface but really are not. There is a hidden agenda. The hidden agenda is conveyed with an ulterior transaction (or a series of ulterior transactions) which is the central core of the game and usually determines the payoff. Payoffs are the not-OK feelings people have at the end of a game.

The origin of games

Psychological games, like other games, are learned in childhood. Children learn them by imitating others or by taking the "roles" that others expect them to play. The game roles are Victim, Persecutor, and Rescuer. It is common for children to see their parents as critical Persecutors and nurturing Rescuers and to see themselves as poor little Victims.

Parents who continually persecute their children are like Critical Dictators. They play games of *Blemish*, which is always finding something wrong, and *Now I've Got You, You S.O.B.*, which is waiting for something to go wrong and then pouncing on the Victim.

When grown up, some children of persecuting parents copy them, imitate their games, and often act as Critical Dictators on the job.

Other children of persecuting parents take the expected roles of Victim or Pacifier, trying to keep peace in the family. This may become their bossing style, and later in life they may still be uncomfortable with conflict and criticism. They may play games such as *Look How Hard I'm Trying* or *Poor Me*.

Still other persons with similar punitive childhood experiences may become Fighter bosses. They may still be fearful, but nevertheless enjoy fighting back. Some become dirty fighters; some decide to play it fair.

Parents who continually rescue their children in the manner of overnurturing caretakers play games such as *Why Don't You*, which is always giving "constructive" advice, and *I'm Only Trying to Help*, which is always being available and giving more helpful advice. Later in life, children with this kind of experience may imitate their parents on the job and become Benevolent Dictators or Supporting Coaches.

If they do not copy a nurturing parent, then they may act out the opposite expected role, once again a Victim, feeling helpless, confused, or scatterbrained.

Parents who are Supportive Critics and Coaches, Liberators rather than jailers, are *not* Dictators. They encourage their children to think analytically, to fight fairly, and to cooperate creatively. This is a very OK combination. People who are fortunate enough to have parents like this play fewer games than the rest of the human race. When they do play them, it is with less intensity, and is therefore less destructive.

The game plan

Every game has a plan for playing. It is much like a plan used in games such as football or chess. It has predictable plays that all players know, though they may not be aware of knowing.

To discover a game plan, the following questions are asked:

- What keeps happening over and over that leaves someone feeling bad?

- How does it start?
- What happens next? And next?
- How does it all end?
- How does each person feel when it ends?

If one or both persons have negative feelings after a repetitive series of transactions, a game has been played. The same is true if one has a bad feeling and the other feels self-righteous.

That which keeps happening over and over again can be described briefly and becomes the name of the game.

There is, for example, the game plan of *Tricky Switches*, which leads to employee resentment. The game starts with a boss who keeps changing procedures. It continues with employees who say things such as "Day after day she keeps changing her mind. First I feel confused because it happens over and over again. Then I feel mad. One of these days I'm going to quit." The quit is the end of the game.

The games of Rapo and Blemish

The first move in a game is called the "con." It is often an ulterior transaction (diagrammed with a dotted line) and is a device to attract another person into joining the game. The con can be sent from any ego state in one person to any ego state in another.

For example, the game of *Rapo* starts when one person makes a verbal statement and gives another person a sexual come-on, hinting at availability. The hint is a Child-to-Child transaction. If the second player responds to the hint and makes an overture, then he or she is "hooked" and the game is on.

The next play in *Rapo* is when the first player switches ego states and "brushes off" the second player indignantly, Parent-to-Child. The second player, while trying to "keep his cool," responds, Child-to-Parent.

The game of RAPO starts when one person gives another person a sexual come-on, hinting at availability. The hint is a Child to Child transaction.

Finally, as the series of transactions comes to a finish, each player in the game experiences an old familiar feeling such as anger, sadness, guilt, confusion, and self-righteousness. This is the payoff. Because of this feeling, each also feels *justified* in reacting in specific ways. Each cashes in the feeling in some way such as sulking, ridiculing, exploding, or saying to themselves something like:

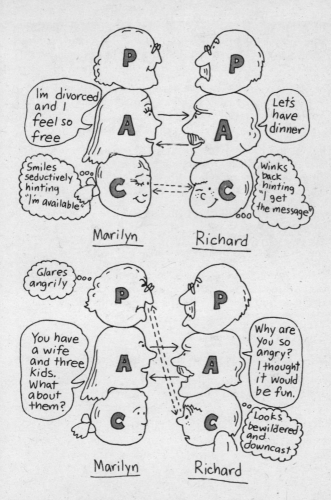

Marilyn (self-righteously) "Forget it. I'm tired of leeches like you. Men are all alike."

Richard (embarrassed and angry) "I can't understand you women! I'm playing poker with the boys tonight anyway."

The game of *Blemish* starts when one person hints that something must be 100% perfect with a remark such as, "I'm going to detail the things I want you to do. Pay close attention." The hint is a Parent-to-Child transaction.

The game continues when the second player responds to the hint by trying very hard, then making one minor mistake. The first player, often from a self-righteous feeling of I'm OK, You're not-OK, points out this blemish.

The second player may then feel depressed, I'm not-OK, You're OK, and explode in anger, or defensively claim, "I'm not a machine. I'm just human. So I make a little mistake once in a while. So what!"

The first player, feeling frustrated and self-righteous, may continue to expect perfection with, "I don't care how long it takes you to do it; just hand it in tomorrow." And on and on.

Games are repetitive. People tend to play the same ones over and over again and may recognize the fact with, "Seems to me, we've been through this hassle before."

Names of the games

Games have names which reflect the theme of the game.

The theme can be spotted by observing what keeps happening over and over again that seems to leave someone feeling not-OK. This theme can then be used as a colloquial name of the game.

For example, a secretary who asks the boss to sign an important letter that has several typing errors yet has to get out on schedule is playing the game of *Kick Me*. *Kick Me* is doing things that invite put-downs. The player attracts others who are willing to be critical and give a kick.

The secretary's ulterior message is "Kick Me for my carelessness." The boss's ulterior message is "Here's your kick. What's the matter with you anyway?" Then the secretary feels sad, "I'm not-OK." The boss feels mad, "You're not-OK."

A sales person who is continually late for appointments with customers and blames the traffic or someone else for being late is playing *If It Weren't For Him* (*Her*). To avoid responsibility, which is the game theme, the player tries to "con" someone else into being sympathetic. The game is played to collect self-righteous feelings.

A boss who continually takes on more and more responsibilities, says "yes" to all demands, comes in early, and works late, sometimes even at lunch-time or on weekends, is playing the game of *Harried*.

Harried is being overly busy, then collapsing with depression, bad back, ulcers, heart attack, and so forth. The *Harried* player often leaves things in a mess for others to straighten out, feeling overburdened and self-righteous while doing so.

Other common on-the-job games are *Cornered*, with the theme, "Damned if I do and damned if I don't"; *Uproar*, with the theme, "You stupid clod, you never do anything right"; and *Let's You and Him (Her) Fight*, with the theme of one person stirring up a fight between others to prove once more that "People are fools."

Games are repetitive because of the game plan each one has. They happen over and over to the same people in similar ways. It is not necessary to know the technical names of all the games. Knowing the theme is sufficient.

Why Don't You . . . Yes, But Games

It takes two or more to play a game. Each has responsibility for it. One person's favorite game may interlock with a complementary game of someone else. The combination of *Why Don't You* and *Yes, But* is an example.

A supervisor who gives a lot of unwanted Parental advice to an employee who turns it down is playing the game of *Why Don't You* . . . (do this, do that, try this, try that).

The other player is playing a complementary game of *Yes, But* (it won't work because . . . and because . . . and because). The basic transaction is diagramed:

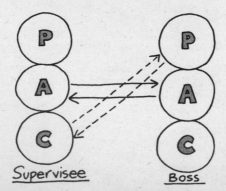

Supervisee (cons by looking helpless): I have a problem . . .

Boss (is hooked and looks helpful): Why don't you try . . .

Supervisee (looking concerned, confused or still helpless): Yes, but that won't work because . . .

Boss: Why don't you . . .

Supervisee: Yes, but . . .

The game goes on and on until the *Why Don't You* boss gives up, feeling frustrated because the seemingly asked for help is not accepted.

At the same time, the *Yes, But* player feels a secret sense of glee. Once more an authority figure has been conned into a game, then put down when responding with the offer of help.

When two supervisors or managers play these two inter-locking games with each other, one is often a subtle Fighter playing *Yes, But . . .* and the other is often a Coach or Pacifier playing *Why Don't You . . .*

Game roles

When people play games they start out in one of the three roles of Persecutor, Rescuer, or Victim and then switch to another of the three.

A subordinate playing *I'm Only Trying To Help You* may act as a Rescuer to a boss and then, if the help is refused, may switch to the Victim role and inwardly complain, "I do all the work, but the boss gets all the glory."

Or, playing the game of *Uproar*, a boss, acting as a Persecutor, may bawl out a subordinate; then, feeling victimized and guilty for exploding, may complain. "No matter what I do, it turns out wrong."

Or a coworker may start off in a Victim position by asking for help with a *Poor Me* game and then, rejecting the

help that is offered, turn Persecutor with, "Stop telling me what to do all the time."

The game roles of Victim, Persecutor, and Rescuer can be diagramed on a triangle. The arrows indicate the way roles may be switched.

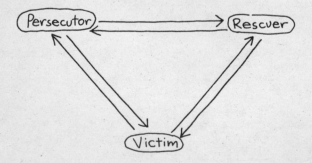

The roles are diagramed this way because people who feel like Victims often seek others who will act as Persecutors and give them a psychological kick. They are not aware of doing this and may, in fact, complain to themselves, "Why does this always happen to me!"

Or Victims may seek others who will act as Rescuers and help them out, over and over and over again. After a number of efforts to make the Victim feel good, the Rescuer may begin to feel like a Victim.

People in the role of Victim are frequently in the I'm not-OK, You're OK position. Their assumption is I'm not-OK and deserve to be rescued or persecuted, You're OK and have the power to rescue or persecute me. This attitude sometimes brings out the worst side of any boss.

Rescuers and Persecutors also reflect their psychological, OK not-OK positions. They may attract people who feel or who act not-OK and unknowingly get caught up in playing the interlocking game roles. For example, Critical Dictators, from their not-OK side, can usually spot a Pacifier or a Fighter to beat upon psychologically.

Collecting psychological stamps

In TA terms, the *feelings* that are collected at the end of a game are called *trading stamps* because they are similar to the kinds of stamps people collect when they buy things such as groceries or gas.

Like having a favorite bossing style, people tend to collect a "favorite" feeling. It isn't always one that feels good, but it's familiar. It's the feeling they have most often when things go wrong. This feeling is usually the same one they had when things went wrong when they were little children.

When collecting stamps, people often say things that include a reference to color. Therefore, stamps are sometimes color-coded: red for anger, green for envy, blue for depression, yellow for fear, gray for indifference, white for self-righteousness.

With anger stamps a person might say, "I'm so mad I can see red," while playing the game, *Now I've Got You, You S.O.B.*

With depression stamps a person might say, "I've got the blues," while playing the game, *Kick Me.*

With envy stamps a person might say, "I'm green with envy," while playing the game, *Let's You and Him Fight.*

With fear stamps a person might say, "I'm too yellow to fight back," while playing the game, *Look How Hard I'm Trying.*

Even if people do not refer to colors when describing their feelings, the feelings often show in some way.

People who collect white purity stamps act blameless if things go wrong. They save feelings of self-righteousness playing games such as *I'm Only Trying To Help.*

People who constantly feel indifferent have lost their zest for color. They see the world as gray and are often seen by others in the same light. "What a drag," they may say.

Instead of collecting negative stamps, some people go for genuine OK feelings that are like 18-carat gold. These are feelings of satisfaction, appreciation, even joy. This kind of collection is most popular with bosses who act from their positive side because they have taken an I'm OK, You're OK position.

Prizes for stamp collecting

When people save up enough negative-feeling stamps they feel entitled to a *prize*. To get the prize they go to a "center" such as a bar or a bedroom, where they can

To get the prize they go to a "center" such as a bar or a bedroom.

cash in their stamps for what the not-OK part of them wants.

- The angry person may feel *justified* in yelling and pounding a desk. The explosion is the prize. It is what the person really wanted.

- The envious person may feel *justified* in gossiping and in undermining someone else.

- The depressed person may feel *justified* in making serious mistakes.

- The fearful person may feel *justified* in doing nothing.

- The self-righteous person may feel *justified* in being overly critical.

Strangely enough, many people are relieved after feeling bad and then acting-out their feelings. But, people around them often feel quite the opposite, and may initiate a new series of games that lead to more not-OKness.

In contrast, people who collect good feelings feel *justified* in having fun and letting others have fun, in sometimes giving others a raise, in being more effective, and in encouraging others to be likewise.

Intensity of games

Games are played at three levels of intensity.

First-degree games involve small collections of stamps. Such games are played in every work and social situation. They are not disastrous. The persons involved, with only a small collection of negative feelings, cash them in for a small prize such as weeping, making a mistake, having a temper tantrum, taking an extra drink, and so forth.

Second-degree game players have more invested in their feelings and in justifying their behavior. The collections they save are larger. Therefore, the prizes they get when cashing in are also larger. Prizes for second-degree game players often include a "quit." Such people may quit school, a marriage, a job. Or they may almost quit life by getting emotionally mixed up, by getting into car accidents, or by getting into serious financial difficulty. They justify quitting because they've "been trying so hard," "they've taken so much," "they are so sick and tired of being bossed around all the time," and so forth.

Third-degree game players "go for broke." They play games as if their lives depended upon the outcome. And they do for these players. They have huge collections of negative feelings because they save them up for years and years. Consequently, they go for the "big" prizes—homicide or suicide. The suicide can be a sudden deliberate act or a slower pattern of eating, drinking, or working too much. The homicide can also be a sudden deliberate act or a slower pattern of encouraging others to overdrink, overeat, or overwork.

Being able to stop games and to deescalate "hard" games into "soft" games that are less destructive are signs of OKness.

Self-discovery 6

Look around your office or home.

What kinds of games are being played?

Who is the Persecutor, the Rescuer, the Victim?

What is the game plan?

Do bad feelings seem to evolve? If so, what kind?

How are the bad feelings cashed in?

What is the prize received?

How about you? What kinds of games do you play?

Is there anything that keeps happening to you over and over again? Write down the moves in your game:

What happens first is: _____

   And then: _____

   And then: _____

How do you feel when the sequence is over?

What do you do next?

When do you feel like a:

Persecutor? _____

Rescuer? _____

Victim? _____

Other people probably see me as a: _____

What happens to your feelings, to the feelings of others?

Do you sometimes feel justified in some kind of behavior?

Do you think something could be done differently?

So what to do

Bosses who want to stop initiating their own games, or who want to stop getting hooked into other people's games, or who want to intervene between two coworkers, need to clearly understand game theory, game plans, game roles, and game payoffs.

They need to be able to interrupt their habitual games and avoid interlocking with the games other people play.

To do this, an uncontaminated Adult is necessary. Your Adult can figure out how you get hooked into games. It can find other options and learn how to cross gaming transactions.

For example, if you get hooked into playing *Yes, But,* the interlocking game is giving "helpful" advice. So the *Yes, But* game is stopped if you don't give advice. You can bounce the problem back to the person who presented it with something like, "What do *you* think would work?"

Other ways to break up a *Yes, But* game include statements such as "I don't know what kind of help I can give you," or "I don't know the best way to solve your problem" when advice is sought.

If you get hooked into a game with a Critical Dictator who plays *Now I've Got You, You S.O.B.*, one way to break it up is to say something like, "I'll think about it," or "That's an interesting point you made."

If you get hooked into a game with an overnurturing Coach who plays *I'm Only Trying To Help You*, you could say something like, "I prefer to do this myself," or "You're supervising me too closely. Please give me some space."

If hooked into a game with a withdrawn Shadow who plays *Don't Bother Me*, you could say something like, "I need some guidelines; are you willing to spend 15 minutes with me on this?" or "I haven't the authority to make this decision. Can we talk it over?"

If hooked into a game with a Fighter who plays *Why Don't You and Him (Her) Fight*, you could say something like, "I prefer not to hear the gossip," or "If there's something you don't like about that person, handle it directly, not through me."

If hooked into a game with a Pacifier who plays *Let's Not Rock the Boat*, you could say something like, "I'd prefer not to fight, but I need to get some clarification," or "I've noticed that when we're honest with each other we often solve problems."

If hooked into a game with a Scatterbrain, you could say something like, "Would you sit down and explain it slowly?" or "What might be the outcome of that plan?" or "What are the variables that need to be thought through?"

You can break up any game if you are willing to give up exaggerating your own strengths and weaknesses and exploiting the strengths and weaknesses of others. The simplest way is to stop putting yourself down and stop putting others down.

Games of effective and efficient bosses

OK bosses, who use the OK parts of their personalities, feel good about themselves and others.

When caught in a game, they stop playing Rescuer—helping those who don't want help.

They stop playing Persecutor—criticizing those who don't improve with it.

They stop playing Victim—acting helpless and dependent when able to solve their own problems.

Instead, they act:

- Creative, as OK Inventor Bosses

- Gutsy, as OK Assertive-Partner Bosses

- Accommodating, as OK Negotiator Bosses

- Responsive, as OK Analyst Bosses
- Noninterfering, as OK Liberator Bosses
- Supportive, as OK Coach Bosses
- Informed, as OK Critic Bosses

The games OK bosses play are usually first-degree and are infrequent. Both effective and efficient bosses know that authenticity is better than game playing.

They know that being straight is better than being devious, that using the positive side of their personality is better than using the negative side. Authenticity beats game playing, is more effective, more efficient, and more fun.

7

Scripts bosses act

Scripts defined

Everyone has a psychological script. It is much like a theatrical script. People tend to live by their scripts without realizing that they do so.

A *psychological script* can be briefly described as a life plan, very much like a dramatic stage production, that an individual feels compelled to act out.

Eric Berne said a person in a script is like someone at a player piano, acting as though he or she created the music and sometimes rising to take a bow or a boo from friends and relatives who also believe that they are hearing the "player's" own tune.

Scripts are preplanned. They are ongoing productions for the dramas of life. They dictate where people are going with their lives and how they are going to get there.

Scripts are played out on various "stages" such as home and work. Some people act out the same script wherever they are. Others change scripts when they change stages. They "act" one way at home and another way at work.

The ways people act are often determined by the culture which, like a director of a drama, says this is the way it's supposed to be. Consequently, people of a specific race, ethnic background, age, sex, and so forth, may be scripted by the culture to certain kinds of jobs with a certain level of authority. OK organizations try to break up this kind of typecasting.

Types of scripts

Any script a person acts out may resemble a trite soap-opera, a wild adventure, a tragedy, a farce, a joyful romance, a comedy, or a dull play that bores the players and would put an audience to sleep.

Individuals have scripts. So do cultures, subcultures, families, and organizations. Even divisions or departments within an organization may be scripted to OKness

or not-OKness. As Shakespeare said, "All the world's
a stage."

The types of scripts that people act out can be classified
as OK and therefore *constructive*; as not-OK and
therefore *destructive*; and as so-so and therefore banal,
or *going nowhere*.

Not-OK scripts. Individual bosses or organizations with
destructive scripts sooner or later injure themselves and
others. They may do it gradually, over an extended
period of time, or with dramatic suddenness.

Destructive scripts are acted out *gradually* with overwork,
overstress, overemphasis on productivity. They are also
played out when bosses, whose passive behavior is due
to indifference or fear, allow destructive people, programs, or services to continue on in an organization.

Tragedy, which is the final curtain of a destructive script,
may occur rather *suddenly* if, for example, disruptive
or dishonest personnel are hired, if physically or mentally
ill employees are not helped, or if employees and
families are geographically moved against their wishes.
Such moves may "seem" useful to the organization but
are often destructive.

People and organizations with destructive scripts are
often indifferent to the suffering of others. They feel little
sense of responsibility for tragedy that may exist at
many levels. They are basically *against* people, including
themselves, rather than for them.

So-so scripts. People and organizations with *so-so
scripts* live a banal existence. Neither destructive nor
constructive, they are merely going nowhere. They avoid
change. They restrict their own growth, limit their own
opportunities, and avoid developing their full potentials.

On the surface they may appear to have OK scripts (after
all, nothing really bad seems to happen) but, in the
long run, they do not accomplish much that is important.
Like squirrels in cages, or animals on a merry-go-round,
they often merely go around in circles.

people and organizations with so-so scripts live a banal existence. Neither destructive or constructive, they are merely going nowhere.

OK scripts. Bosses and organizations with *OK scripts* are concerned about the world and its people as well as those on the job or at home. They know that all people, including themselves, have value and treat them accordingly.

Bosses with OK scripts have a measure of greatness which may or may not be recorded in the mass media. They know that getting billed as a "star" may or may not indicate an OK script. Bosses in OK scripts can be spotted because they act from the plus side of their personalities. Other people like sharing the stage with them. Their own bosses like them as well as their subordinates.

Bosses with OK scripts know who they are as well as what they do. They work actively against situations that contribute to poverty, disease, discrimination and other tragedies that lead to unhealthiness and unhappiness. They are committed to leaving the world stage a somewhat better place for having been part of it.

The origin of scripts

Scripts are unknowingly selected in early years. They *begin* to develop in the womb or soon after birth. If pregnancy is wanted, if the genes of both parents are satisfactory, if the mother is physically and emotionally healthy, if the birth is normal, if the parents are pleased with the sex and appearance of the child, then the child *is likely to begin life feeling OK.*

Children who are cared for properly, who receive positive attention, and who are encouraged to think for themselves are likely to continue feeling OK. They tend to select a constructive I'm OK, You're OK script and later in life become OK bosses.

On the other hand, if a child is not wanted, if something goes wrong during pregnancy or birth, if it is "just one more mouth to feed," if the parents feel resentful, frustrated, or angry at the responsibility, or disappointed in the sex or appearance of the child, the child is likely to begin feeling not-OK and to select a destructive script that matches the feeling.

Many children get mixed messages and conclude they're partly OK and partly not-OK. They tend to fluctuate in their performance and in their feelings of esteem. They often feel that whatever they do is not quite good enough.

Later in life such people may switch back and forth between the superiority positions of I'm OK, You're not-OK and the anxious, depressed position of I'm not-OK, You're OK. They often act out their lives in a so-so banal script, choosing a dead-end job that also goes nowhere.

If a child feels it is "just one more mouth to feed," it is likely to begin feeling not-OK and to select a destructive script that matches the feeling.

The scripting program

Traditions that are passed down to others, whether the traditions are related to jobs or personal life, often are "scripting" messages from parental authority figures who once served as bosses. The scripting process is a program for life that, unknowingly, children adopt for themselves.

Children select their scripts when they are often too young to do so. First they have unique experiences. Then they make decisions based on the experiences. These specifics lead them to their generalized psychological positions. Later in life they act out in some way to reinforce the early decision.

One common scripting experience is being criticized frequently for not getting perfect grades in school, for not doing things perfectly. Children scripted this way may decide that unless they are perfect they won't be acceptable. Their psychological position is likely to be I'm not quite OK, They're OK. In later life their script behavior is trying and trying and trying to be perfect, yet never succeeding and feeling like a loser when criticized.

Another common scripting experience is when children lose a parent by death, desertion, or divorce. Such children may decide, "I won't get close to people again. They may leave me." Their psychological position becomes I'm not-OK, You're not-OK. The script behavior is one of withdrawing from others or, without awareness, selecting people who will leave as the parent once did. The withdrawing is likely to be from those of the same sex as the parent who left. So, too, the selecting of people who will leave.

Other scripting experiences often include specific details that are related to working. A Parental message "Women's place is in the home" may create guilt feelings in the Child ego state of the woman who wants to work. If she has a boss who also had the same scripting, such a boss may "hint," from the Parent ego state, that she should be home, not working on a paid job. Thus, the early childhood experience is reinforced.

Another common script related to working is a Parental message that "Men are supposed to be the boss." Some men agree, choose the position, and are effective bosses. Others may not want the responsibility. They may feel that it's OK for them to have a woman boss. Yet if they make such a statement to their peers, the response they get may be one of disbelief.

Theatrical factors in people's scripts

All scripts call for *producers*. Parents are the original producers in each person's life, but there are others. The producers are usually the "big" bosses. They may be on-stage directing the show, or off-stage directing the director. They often delegate authority for hiring the characters, setting the scene, funding the production, and advising on promotion. Yet the power is there and is interpreted by others as OK or not-OK.

All scripts also call for *characters*. Traditionally, these are the dramatic roles of Victim, Persecutor, and Rescuer. These basic roles are acted out as stereotypes. They are seen by audiences as Dictators, Coaches, Shadows, Fighters, Innovators, Pacifiers, or Analysts. The roles can be acted out from the plus side of the personality, or the minus side, or intermittently from both sides.

Subordinates on the job are often perceived as *supporting characters*. As such, they are likely to have peripheral positions with inconspicuous desks over to one side so that they are not on center stage. They are also expected to "back up" those in the field or in the head office.

Dialogue is part of every script. Dialogue includes verbal and nonverbal transactions. It reveals how the characters feel about themselves and others—as being OK or not-OK. The dialogue is made up of complementary, crossed, and ulterior transactions. The strokes that people give become obvious during the play, and they are authentic or phony lines.

The *scenes* and *acts* in the drama are the "games people play." Games are so often repetitive that they sometimes reflect the theme of the total drama. During a game, the characters and their roles are being acted out. Stamps are collected and cashed in for dramatic prizes. The script moves on to a climax, a denouement, and final curtain. The audience applauds, boos, or acts indifferent.

Even a detail such as *lighting* may be part of the script. For example, a Shadow boss will tend to avoid the spotlight. Fighter and Inventor bosses may "upstage" others to get it.

The *scenery* is the way a situation is decorated, the furnishings and equipment that are used. It is not uncommon for people to speak of wanting a "change of scenery." This often implies they'd prefer a different stage setting, different characters, and a different drama than the one they are presently acting out. Scenery varies. It ranges from bleak unattractiveness to exciting vividness.

One organization changed its scenery without researching the effect of color. The three shades of orange on the wall were too overpowering. Complaints, errors, absenteeism, and personnel turnover increased radically. The scenery contributed to a poor show.

Another organization changed its setting by adding lively colorful carpeting, clever wall murals, and wide open

spaces. Employees were given some freedom to decorate their own scene. It was a fun, creative stage to be on, and the scenery contributed to a good show.

Psychological positions and script themes

One way to look at script and script themes is through the OK positions and how they affect relationships with others. Each script has a theme. Week after week these themes can be spotted by others who are observant.

Confident (I'm OK, You're OK) bosses tend to get along with people by being trustworthy and authentic. Confident bosses might have script themes such as "from one success to another," "acquiring friends not enemies," and "being responsible and fun."

Superiority (I'm OK, You're not-OK) bosses tend to get rid of people by putting them off or putting them down.

Themes of Superiority bosses include such things as attacking the underdog, criticizing the superdog, confusing the middle dog.

Themes of Superiority bosses include such things as "attacking the underdog," "criticizing the super dog," and "confusing the middle dog."

Depressed ('Im not-OK, You're OK) bosses tend to get away from people. Themes of Depressed bosses include: "never doing anything quite right," "always getting the short end of the stick," "trying hard on unimportant things," "being mediocre," and "getting criticized."

Hopeless (I'm not-OK, You're not-OK) bosses tend to give up on people by not expecting anything positive from them or from themselves. Themes of Hopeless bosses include "not getting anything done," "making major mistakes," "driving people crazy," "giving up," and "missing the boat."

Recognizing a script

One way to *recognize* a script is to become aware of who continues to play what role. For example, some people always get themselves into hot water. Or they get the cold freeze. In either case, they act out a Victim role time and time again. They may complain, "Why does this always happen to me?" or "If it weren't for . . . I'd be able to get my work done," or "No matter what I do it turns out wrong," or "Why is everyone always picking on me?"

Others seem to be frequently cast as Rescuers. They may also complain, "I'm willing to work overtime, but no one seems to want my help," or "Why don't people listen to me?" or "With my kind of experience, I know best, so I'll do it."

Dramas also require Persecutors—villains who create Victims for Rescuers to rescue. Persecutors may also complain, "If I've told you once, I've told you a dozen times!" or "I don't understand how you can be so stupid."

Although some people are more subtle than others in the roles they play, all people act at times as though they were reading lines that fit the parts and were written by someone else.

Another way to identify a script is to ask oneself the question, "What happens to people like me?" The "what happens" is the script.

This question can also be useful for discovering scripts that business firms or other organizations might have, "What happens to organizations like this?" or "What seems to go on over and over again, like the theme of a drama?"

Another way of getting some insight into the script is to consider what the logical conclusions are if a person, or an organization, continues to act as it now does. The "logical conclusion" is like a final curtain, or like a curtain falling between acts—such as in the case of a merger.

Self-discovery 7

To discover your script, use your Adult and the intuitive part of your Child and ask yourself the questions:

- What happens to people like me?

- If I go on as I now am, what will be the logical conclusion?

- If I were to die today, what would my epitaph say about me as a boss?

- Does my script seem to be constructive? Destructive? Or going nowhere?

To discover the script of your organization, use the above sentences again, changing the pronouns to nouns to fit your situation. Then ask:

- Do any characters need changing? If so, who?

- What else needs to change to get a better show on the road?

So what to do

The things that happen to the same people, over and over again, are brief scenes in their scripts. These things are usually related in some way to what happened in their childhood. They are like replays of earlier scenes. Sometimes this is constructive and OK.

In contrast, some people, instead of living by their own scripts, copy their parents and live according to their parents' scripts. These are people who constantly function from a Parent ego state or from an Adult which is contaminated by Parent traditions. Sometimes this is OK, sometimes part of the script needs to be "rewritten" for more OKness.

For rewriting a script, imagine yourself as a young child on a stage. See again the characters that were on stage with you, the dialogue and action, the kind of show it was. Were you in the spotlight or not? If so, in what way? If not, why not? In retrospect, do you like the way it was?

Now, see yourself on one or more of the stages on which you act in your current life. Who's there? What's the drama going on? Is it OK, not-OK, or merely banal?

Next, imagine yourself as working on an OK stage, dialoguing with OK transactions, living out a good show—both as boss and as subordinate. Is there anything you'd need to do differently?

Changing a script often requires a *redecision* of that which was decided in childhood. Whereas childhood decisions may have survival value at the time they are made, they frequently do not apply in later life. Nor do all cultural and parental traditions.

Bosses who want to increase their OKness and the OKness of others are willing to change negative decisions that are "ancient history." They are willing to let go of the past in favor of new positive decisions made for the here and now.

Effective and efficient scripting

The OK *effective* bosses are those who do the right thing, who know their personal script and use the constructive parts of it.

They also know what their organizational script is all about, what it's doing to people and why. They produce, direct, and act in the situation in such a way that it turns out to be a good show in which people want to participate.

The OK *efficient* bosses are those who do things right. They keep a good show going. They fire or reeducate incompetent characters who were poorly chosen. They redecorate the situation with more stimulating scenery. They develop new dialogue to replace banal cliches and advertising slogans. They update going-nowhere procedures. They take time to rehearse a scene before an important meeting or sale.

Bosses who have not-OK scripts will expect the show to collapse somehow and, knowingly or unknowingly, may contribute to it.

Bosses in so-so banal scripts will expect the show to do only moderately well. They will not develop sufficient skill and creativity—in themselves or in others—to put on a first-rate performance.

Bosses who are winners, who are in the I'm OK, You're OK position, will have a constructive script and a successful show. They will be well liked personally and professionally and applauded in one way or another for their positive bossing style.

Bosses who are winners, will have a constructive script and a successful show. They will be applauded in one way or another for their positive bossing style.

8

Time
for
OK
contracts

Theory of contracts

OK bosses are interested in becoming winners, or extending their winning streak. They are also concerned about enhancing the winning characteristics of their employees.

In TA terms, OK bosses can establish *contracts* to achieve these goals. Contracts are plans of action to which a person is committed. They contain details of what, when, where, how, and with whom. They can be made with oneself or with others.

A contract is an agreement to *do something about something*, such as to complete a delayed report, or to confront an employee who is continually late, or to take time out for a vacation, or to work over the budget until it balances, or to quit smoking.

Types of contracts

There are three areas in which contracts can be made.

Contracts can be established to *change behavior*; for example, to stop procrastinating and to start completing projects as scheduled.

Contracts can be established to *change feelings*; for example, to stop feeling like a Victim when criticized, and to start evaluating criticism realistically.

Contracts can be established to *decrease psychosomatic symptoms*, such as overweight or high blood pressure, and to start respecting one's own body and feelings.

Many people refuse to make valid contracts because of a feeling of "I can't." Consequently, such people don't reach their goals. They are tied to destructive or going-nowhere banal scripts. The purpose of learning how to make contracts is to increase personal OKness and the OKness of others.

Requirements of contracts

Contracts need to be clear, precise, and direct. They also need to be based on realistic goals which can be reached by realistic means.

For instance, a realistic contract can be made about looking more attractive, but it is not realistic to expect, at age fifty, to turn back the clock and look like a person of twenty. Realistic contracts can be made about feeling better, but it is not realistic for people to expect to feel better without changing their life style, or job, or the way they structure their time.

To achieve a goal, some kind of external or internal change is necessary. The willingness to change is thus a major requirement. Many bosses are for change, but they want other people to change rather than changing themselves. Yet in every contract some kind of personal change is necessary.

To improve communication on the job, a boss might need to stop blaming others for "not understanding," to take responsibility for his or her own side of the transactions, to experiment with being straightforward and direct rather than being indirect and playing games.

"What could *I* do differently to achieve my goal?" is a continuing question for the OK boss.

Making personal contracts

There is a five-step questioning process for successfully making a contract.

First comes the establishment of a goal with the question, "What do I want that would enhance my life or job?" This is recognizing the fact that personal goals are OK to have and so are goals about a job situation.

Next comes the question, "What would I need to change so that I could reach my goal? This is recognizing that personal change, not just changing others, is necessary.

Of course, others may change in the process but that's not the focus of this question.

Third is, "What would I be willing to do to make the change happen?" This is recognizing that change in a situation usually starts with one person who is willing to do something about something, instead of just sitting around complaining and blaming.

The next step is to ask, "How would others know when I have effected the change?" This is recognizing that feedback from others is an effective reinforcement process.

The fifth step is to question, "How might I sabotage or undermine myself so that I would not achieve my goals? This is recognizing how inner dialogue, or transactions with others, or games that are played, or scripts that are acted out, might interfere with the successful completion of a contract.

The fifth step is to question "How might I sabotage or undermine myself so that I would not achieve my goals.

Making contracts with others

A similar process is required in order to effect change between two people or to change something in an employee that may need changing.

In this case, the contract-making process often uses statements followed by questions. It might go as follows:

"Stan, a *goal* has been set by the company for us to increase production 12%. Would you be willing to agree with this goal?"

If Stan answers "yes," the contract-making can continue. If not, then further discussion on the goal is necessary until Stan agrees.

Next comes, "Stan, is there anything that needs changing so that this goal could be reached?" Discussion would then follow.

Third comes, "I'm wondering if there's something you could do, Stan, and would be willing to do to make this change happen?" More discussion.

Then, "What kind of evaluation or feedback do you think is needed so that others in the organization would be aware of the change?" Again, more talk.

The fifth step is, "How might the goal and the process be sabotaged?" or "Who might do what that would interfere with success?"

When making contracts with other people, it is essential that each point be discussed in order and that time be available for discussion.

Bosses who are overly busy, who play the game of *Harried*, who claim they "don't have enough time" to think about it or talk it through, are sabotaging themselves, their employees, and their organization.

A caution on contracts

Sometimes bosses and employees, in a flurry of enthusiasm, make unrealistic contracts. Like people who make New Year's Eve resolutions, they do not evaluate their commitment to change. Consequently, their good intentions are short-lived.

Writing down the answers to each of the five contract steps is one way to avoid this kind of failure. It is important, however, to continually review and evaluate the progress of the contract. Sometimes the Parent and Child ego states interfere with this Adult process.

A person's Parent might undermine the process by sending messages such as, "Keep on working"; in other words, "Don't stop to think about what you're working on." The Child might undermine the process by responding, "See how hard I'm working"; in other words, "See how obedient I am by not questioning the value of what I do."

Unless the boss is alert, these messages from the Parent and Child can contaminate the Adult decision to make and keep a contract. Writing things down, then periodically reviewing them, is an effective way to sabotage the potential saboteur.

Time-structuring and contracts

People's poor management of time often interferes with making effective contracts. They may complain, "Changing would take too much time," or "I don't have time to think about it now."

According to TA, there are six ways that bosses and subordinates structure time. These are: activities, withdrawal, rituals, pastimes, games, and intimacy.

Activities are commonly thought of as work. Seemingly, a person goes to work to perform an activity, yet within the work situation the other five forms of time-structuring also occur. For example, a sudden flurry of paper-shuffling when a boss comes by often indicates a game. Or a far-away look when holding a report may indicate a withdrawal into the fantasy of a fishing trip rather than the thoughtful study of the report.

Generally speaking, time spent in activities is positive—things get done. These things may not always be the "right" thing, however. Just because some employees are busy doesn't mean they are working effectively or efficiently.

Activities are negative if people are into a "work, work, work" script without considering why. The constant use of time for activities can create a sterile emotional environment. People want and need other forms of time-structuring. The old cliche, "All work and no play makes Jack a dull boy," is all too true.

Withdrawal, as a form of time-structuring, can be physical or emotional. It can be used as a technique to avoid people or to avoid solving a problem, or it can be used in a more positive way to re-create self-esteem and energy or to develop solutions to problems.

If a person withdraws physically by leaving the room or hanging up the phone, this obviously affects others and communication is cut off. Changing the subject or day-dreaming while nodding "uh huh" have the same effect.

If a person withdraws physically by leaving the room, this obviously affects others and communication is cut off.

Psychological withdrawal is a positive act when the time is used for planning, reflecting, creating, or recovering from the impact of overstimulation. It is negative when its purpose is to wallow in self-pity, or indulge in feelings of hostility. It is also negative if a problem needs to be solved, not avoided.

Rituals are the highly predictable stereotyped transactions such as "Hello," "Hello," "How are you?" "Fine."

OK bosses use such kinds of rituals in a positive way to give "maintenance" strokes to employees. The recipients usually give back similar ritualistic strokes. Each is likely to feel recognized.

In some situations, a "hello" from a boss carries a lot of weight. However, overly busy bosses, playing games such as *Harried Executive*, sometimes act as though rituals were a "waste of time." This is from their not-OK side. Rituals, as minimal forms of recognition, are necessary in most working situations.

Negatively used, rituals may be devoid of emotion. They may be only words that lack a caring dimension. When this is the case, both subordinates and bosses may feel hungry for "something more." It is not uncommon for "top" bosses to speak of their lonely position. Even for them, rituals are not enough. For most employees, the rituals of gold watches at retirement, or cocktail parties at Christmas, or cups of coffee day after day after day are not a good enough substitute for authentic contact.

Pastimes are extended conversations at a somewhat casual level about subjects such as sports, weather, cars, kids, vacations, and so forth. They often are extensions of rituals. For example, during the ritual of a coffee break, "pastiming" is common. In fact, it is so deeply ingrained in many work situations that not to have it would be interpreted by some as the breaking of a "sacred" tradition.

Pastimes are a positive use of time when they enable people to get acquainted with each other or when they break the monotony of a boring job or the tension of a difficult one. From the other side, pastimes can "eat up so much time" that they may interfere with "getting the job done." They may also contribute to the maintenance of superficial relationships or can lead into psychological game playing.

Games are usually an unproductive use of time, a series of transactions with an ulterior purpose. When games are over, someone is likely to have collected a bad-feeling stamp. Games interfere with problem solving and decision making. They decrease feelings of loyalty and the sense of trust.

Sometimes it is useful to play a mild form of a game, especially with someone who is a second- or third-degree player and who doesn't want to change. But, generally speaking, games are a waste of time.

OK bosses learn how to be discreet if they prefer one employee over another.

Intimacy is the sixth way people may structure their time. Intimacy, in the TA sense, does not refer to sexual contact, which may be a pastime or a game. Intimacy refers to affectionate and appreciative feelings. It involves open, honest relationships with a minimum of ulterior transactions.

Although intimacy feels good for those who are involved, it may be negative to those who observe it, or sense it, in others. They may feel jealous and see themselves "left out" of the relationship.

OK bosses learn how to be discreet if they prefer one employee over another. They know that to be open and intimate with one may be perceived as "playing favorites" by others. This usually has a demoralizing effect on those who feel themselves not so esteemed.

Therefore, whenever possible, OK bosses express appreciation to many employees. Their essential openness and lack of game playing increases the OKness in others.

Self-discovery 8

To increase your OKness, experiment with a contract:

- Is there anything you want that would enhance your life and job?

- What would need changing?

- What are you willing to do that would effect the change?

- How would others perceive the changes?

- How might you sabotage yourself?

Now do an ego-state review to discover how you structure your time:

- What would be your Parent's opinion about the way you use your time?

- How does your Adult compute your use of time?

- What does your Child feel about your use of time?

- By any chance, do you need a contract to restructure your time and take more time out for *you* to increase your OKness?

So what to do

It's not easy to contract to change oneself; it's not easy to get someone else involved in changing; but both can be done. An effective way to get into contracting is to start with small goals and achieve them before moving on to something larger.

For instance, Martha has established a reasonable goal; she wants to become a more dynamic speaker. To achieve this goal, she has to change her habit of mumbling and gesturing wildly. She can make this change happen by taking a public-speaking course at the local evening school. Also, she will need to practice in front of a mirror. Others will know the goal has been achieved when they see her speak at the next sales meeting. Martha may sabotage herself by being "too busy" or "too scared" or "too lazy" to attend the public speaking course.

Martha's contract is specific and has a definite plan of action. It is not global or a once-and-for-all commitment. Martha, like other successful people, continually builds on her earlier, sometimes smaller successes.

By learning and applying the skills of contracting, you can take more definite control of your life.

You can contract to listen with your Adult to your own inner dialogue. You may hear an inner voice using your name and saying something like, "What's the matter with you,_____? Can't you do anything right!" This is your inner Parent beating upon your Child. Or, you may hear something like, "I just can't do it. I wouldn't dare try." This is your apologetic, fearful Child avoiding responsibility. Your Adult can effectively referee between this top dog and under dog dialogue.

You can also contract to transact more openly, using complementary transactions when possible, and crossing game transactions when they become harmful.

You can contract to use your time for you. You don't *always* have to say "yes" when you want to say "no."

You can choose who to spend time with in activities and intimacy and who to avoid.

You can decide what kind of a boss to be *now*. Next year. Five years from now. Also, what kind of a job to have now. Next year. Five years from now.

Look at what needs changing. Decide what you're willing to do, set up a time schedule, and do it.

Effective and efficient time-structuring

Bosses in constructive scripts may on occasion use all forms of time-structuring. However, the greatest part of their time is devoted to activities and intimacy. When they make their "to do" list, they give priority to important issues and the people they care about. They manage their time well.

Bosses in constructive scripts may on occasion use all forms of time structuring. However, the greatest part of their time is devoted to activities and intimacy. They manage their time well.

They are willing to make contracts with others which will enhance the quality of this life.

They avoid lengthy "pastiming" and going-nowhere rituals which are characteristic of people who have banal scripts. They use withdrawal, rituals, and pastimes only when appropriate, not as a way of killing time.

OK bosses seldom get caught up in the endless games that are played by people in destructive scripts. When they do, they get out of them in OK ways.

Effective bosses know their priorities and set contracts to achieve them. They care about people, including themselves. *Efficient* bosses show their caring in OK ways. They move out toward others with confidence, using their positive side.

The OK boss

The Critic type of boss gives up being a not-OK Critical Dictator in favor of being an OK Informed Critic.

The Coach type of boss gives up being a not-OK Benevolent Dictator in favor of being an OK Supportive Coach.

The Shadow type of boss gives up being a not-OK Loner in favor of being an OK Liberator.

The Analyst type of boss gives up being a not-OK Computer in favor of being an OK Communicator.

The Pacifier type of boss gives up being a not-OK Milquetoast in favor of being an OK Negotiator.

The Fighter type of boss gives up being a not-OK Punk in favor of being an OK Partner.

The Inventor type of boss gives up being a not-OK Scatterbrain in favor of being an OK Innovator.

All effective and efficient bosses are flexible. They figure out the best ways to maximize their own potential and the potential of those around them. They all have the psychological position,

"I'm basically OK and,
basically,
So are you!"

ABOUT THE ILLUSTRATOR

JOHN TROTTA is an award-winning illustrator, designer and author who lives in New York. He produces children's books, school books, adult books, posters, record covers and advertisements. He is also a regular contributor to *The New York Times* and *Woman's Day*.

Bantam
On Psychology

☐	FRITZ, Martin Shepard	2202	• $1.95
☐	SIMULATIONS OF GOD: THE SCIENCE OF BELIEF, John C. Lilly, M.D.	2442	• $2.25
☐	TRANSCENDENTAL MEDITATION, Jack Forem	2675	• $1.95
☐	IN AND OUT THE GARBAGE PAIL, Fritz Perls	6369	• $1.95
☐	THE GESTALT APPROACH & EYE WITNESS TO THERAPY, Fritz Perls	6414	• $1.95
☐	BREAKING FREE, Nathaniel Branden	8031	• $1.50
☐	PSYCHOSOURCES, A Psychology Resource Catalog, Evelyn Shapiro, ed.	8501	• $5.00
☐	THE PSYCHOLOGY OF SELF-ESTEEM: A New Concept of Man's Psychological Nature, Nathaniel Branden	10189	• $1.95
☐	WHAT DO YOU SAY AFTER YOU SAY HELLO? Eric Berne, M.D.	10251	• $2.25
☐	GESTALT THERAPY VERBATIM, Fritz Perls	10470	• $2.25
☐	PSYCHO-CYBERNETICS AND SELF-FULFILLMENT, Maxwell Maltz, M.D.	10535	• $1.95
☐	THE FIFTY-MINUTE HOUR, Robert Lindner	10537	• $1.95
☐	AWARENESS: exploring, experimenting, experiencing, John O. Stevens	10562	• $2.25
☐	THE DISOWNED SELF, Nathaniel Branden	10612	• $1.95
☐	PSYCHOANALYSIS AND RELIGION, Erich Fromm	11192	• $1.75
☐	WHEN I SAY NO, I FEEL GUILTY, Manuel Smith	11400	• $2.25

Buy them at your local bookstore or use this handy coupon for ordering:

Bantam Book Catalog

Here's your up-to-the-minute listing of every book currently available from Bantam.

This easy-to-use catalog is divided into categories and contains over 1400 titles by your favorite authors.

So don't delay—take advantage of this special opportunity to increase your reading pleasure.

Just send us your name and address and 25¢ (to help defray postage and handling costs).

BANTAM BOOKS, INC.
Dept. FC, 414 East Golf Road, Des Plaines, Ill. 60016

Mr./Mrs./Miss_____
                            (please print)

Address_____

City_____State_____Zip_____

Do you know someone who enjoys books? Just give us their names and addresses and we'll send them a catalog too!

_____

Mr./Mrs./Miss_____

Address_____

City_____State_____Zip_____

_____

Mr./Mrs./Miss_____

Address_____

City_____State_____Zip_____

FC—6/77